God, Can I Complain?

The Cancer Patient's Book of Jeremiah's Laments

JAMES ADERMAN

NORTHWESTERN PUBLISHING HOUSE
Milwaukee, Wisconsin

God, Can I Complain?

The Cancer Patient's Book of Jeremiah's Laments

JAMES ADERMAN

Northwestern Publishing House
N16W23379 Stone Ridge Dr., Waukesha WI 53188-1108
www.nph.net
© 2024 by Northwestern Publishing House
Published 2024
Printed in the United States of America
ISBN 978-0-8100-2950-7
ISBN 978-0-8100-2951-4 (e-book)

24 25 26 27 28 29 30 31 32 33   10 9 8 7 6 5 4 3 2 1

To my grandchildren:
Ellie, Cadence, Hudson,
Silas, Thatcher, Vera, Everett,
Gunnar, Lincoln, and Miles.
May you always treasure God's grace.

FOREWORD

Share the story! Make it real and human. We are familiar with the principle. Reporters go to the site of breaking news and look for a witness to tell the story. They put a microphone in front of someone who has seen what happened. The words from someone who has been there and witnessed compel the story.

That principle stands behind this series of books entitled When Cancer Comes. We wanted to tell the story of cancer patients who struggled with their faith when the voice of Jesus seemed to evaporate in the heat of suffering. How did they find strength and comfort when cancer, like a hot coal, sizzled comfort away? We looked for writers who could tell their stories so that others could grow and find strength. We wanted their stories to be real and human.

Each author settled on a specific section of Scripture to help structure the story and message. One focused on Job, another on Paul, and another on Jeremiah. Each of these biblical characters had a special point to make while enduring pain and misery. Job wondered why God sent him so much suffering. Paul endured much but found a reason even to boast in his suffering. Jeremiah complained about his suffering and the suffering he saw around him.

These trials are not uncommon for cancer patients, so we asked the authors to tell their stories. They have been in the doctors' offices to hear the word *cancer*. They either have experienced the chemotherapy and weaknesses or have seen a loved one struggle with them. They matched their personal stories to these biblical characters and found ways to coax faith and courage to grow.

In the soil of their dark days, God's promises nurtured the flower of faith.

Our prayer is that their stories help you water the flower of your faith using God's promises when your faith droops under each challenge.

John Braun, editor

Contents

Because of the Lord's great love we are not consumed, for his compassions never fail. They are new every morning; great is your faithfulness. I say to myself, "The Lord is my portion; therefore I will wait for him."

Lamentations 3:22-24

Introduction
DECEMBER 10, 2010

Seven days before my urologist took a biopsy of my prostate.

Before that were several years of frequent prostate-specific anti-gen (PSA) tests. Test after test showed PSA numbers were on the rise—and the pace was quickening. It took less time for my PSA number to jump from 6 to 7 than from 4 to 5. Although a rising PSA number does not indicate that cancer exists, it does signal that something unhealthy is happening.

We set up the December 10 appointment prior to the biopsy. The doctor insisted that Sharon, my wife of 37 years, accompany me. "That way, if there is cancer, I won't have to explain the situation twice," he said. "And, if there is no cancer, the two of you can go out for a nice lunch."

Sharon and I arrived 15 minutes ahead of the appointment. Sharon's nervousness showed in her conversation about a rapid succession of trivial topics: "I hope it doesn't snow today. I have shopping to do later. What should I get for supper? Would you like ham? Hamburgers? I'm worried about my oven. It doesn't seem to heat well."

My nervousness showed in a lack of conversation. Long inhales and longer exhales spoke in ways words could not.

Sharon and I squeezed our hands together to invite Jesus to wait with us. We claimed Isaiah's description of our Savior as the "Mighty God" (Isaiah 9:6). The Spirit had featured that piece of Scripture at the midweek Advent service two days before.

Then we talked about Zephaniah 3:17, another part of the Advent message that week: "The LORD your God is with you, the Mighty Warrior who saves. He will take great delight in you; in his love he will no longer rebuke you, but will rejoice over you with singing."

God did quiet us with the mention of his love. The thought of his rejoicing over us with singing comforted us.

"Jim," the office nurse summoned. Her tone was both a command and a question.

Sharon and I cast a glance in the other's direction. Faint smiles flickered across resolute faces. In unison, we sucked in another deep breath, rose from our seats, clasped hands, and followed our guide out of the waiting area down a long, bright hallway.

The nurse welcomed us into a stark, windowless exam room. She settled us into the barely comfortable aluminum and fabric chairs. The paper that covered exam table, as well as the white metal cupboards and countertops, dressed the room with an antiseptic aura. "The doctor will be with you shortly," she promised. Then, ghostlike, she was gone.

We waited in silence, staring into the nothingness that took the place of the opposite wall. Our fingers intertwined, released, and then intertwined again. They never found a comfortable position. Meanwhile, our hearts called on the Spirit to translate our jumbled prayer thoughts into petitions our Father would understand.

The wait was not long. Within two minutes the doctor whirred into the room. His graying hair needed a comb. His tie hung loose below his unbuttoned collar. He smiled as he shook our hands. Then he plopped into the wheeled office chair that he pulled from the small desk in the corner of the room.

He seemed ready to begin his well-practiced explanation about the prostate, the way its cancer is diagnosed, and, finally, the results of my biopsy. His matter-of-fact tone testified that he had honed this conversation over a quarter century. He had developed an approach that minimized questions, allayed fears, and prepared cancer-afflicted men for the "what now" discussion.

"How are you doing today?" he asked. His question was more a courtesy, a way to begin his presentation, than a request for information.

"I'll feel better once I know what the test showed," Sharon responded.

The physician's face softened into that of a caring friend. We heard a muted, understanding sigh. He reached for a piece of paper from the packet in his lap and handed us the report on the biopsy. He departed from his script.

> "I'm sorry. The biopsy has discovered cancer in the prostate." He was direct yet sympathetic.

"I'm sorry. The biopsy has discovered cancer in the prostate." He was direct yet sympathetic. He paused for a long moment. His news required time to become our reality.

During that pause, I realized that another companion had joined me on my travel toward life's end: cancer. It joined the two broken arms and one broken wrist, the removed appendix and gallbladder, the allergy to penicillin, the poor eyesight, the numerous body glitches due to aging, and the balding head. It became the newest addition to my medical conditions that testify—most every day in some way—I will not live here forever. A cancer diagnosis, however, doesn't just mumble that I am mortal. It screams. It intimidates. It annoys. It torments.

I assume you have opened this book because you too travel with cancer. Or you care about someone who does.

Cancer is an obnoxious seatmate on a 15-hour overseas flight. It's the red-faced screaming one-year-old. The plus-size traveler who intrudes into your seat space. The kid who vomits his airline supper on you. The perspiration-fouled seat neighbor who insists on leaning toward you while carrying on his incessant chatter.

Cancer is worse than an annoying airline passenger. It can be the radicalized bomb builder who threatens to bring the plane down in a fireball.

> In this book, we will learn from the prophet Jeremiah about complaining. Jeremiah is the Bible's premier complainer.

Cancer provides those who travel with it ample fuel for complaint. An agonizing sense of unfairness accompanies cancer. Nightmare fears haunt this diagnosis. Its treatment usually involves discomfort that shoves toward distress. Oncology personnel may seem apathetic. Family and friends may stumble in their support. Those with cancer may assume they need to be strong for others, even when they are struggling to be strong for themselves. Cancer often tortures its victims with the reality of their mortality along with the pain and discomfort.

In this book, we will learn from the prophet Jeremiah about complaining. Jeremiah is the Bible's premier complainer. Journey along with me as we learn from him and the God we share. Along that path, we will discover how to wrestle with cancer's unfairness.

We will begin by introducing ourselves to Jeremiah, the mission God gave him, and the challenges he faced. We will consider the reasons why we feel our complaints are justified. Then we will tackle the answers to questions that will help us wrangle the blessings out of our complaints. Here are the four questions we'll address: Where am I focusing my attention? Who directs what I think? Do I talk more than I listen? Am I placing my confidence in my strength or in God's strength?

Prayer

God of grace, through the prophet Jeremiah, you assured the rebellious people of Jerusalem, "Only if the heavens above can be measured and the foundations of the earth below be searched out will I reject all the descendants of Israel because of all they have done" (Jeremiah 31:37). Comfort me and all who are suffering because of cancer with your unalterable commitment that your love will never desert us. Point us not only to the heavens and the foundations of the earth but also to your Son, Jesus, as the proof of your commitment to us. Amen.

Chapter 1
JEREMIAH'S MISSION

I don't like to spend much time in the books of Jeremiah and Lamentations. Reading a few verses now and then is fine. Consuming multiple chapters in one sitting? That's like trudging through waist-deep snow in a blizzard. These books are depressing.

In Jeremiah's prophecies, the balance between God's rightful judgment on his rebellious people and his never-ending commitment to love them stacks on the judgment side of the scale. The gospel shines there, but it rarely peeks out from the storm clouds of God's roiling wrath. Those peeks are so refreshing and astonishing, perhaps because of the concentration on God's judgments.

> The prophet Jeremiah did not have cancer, but God appointed him to serve as a spiritual oncologist to a people who did have cancer, a terminal cancer.

The prophet Jeremiah did not have cancer, but God appointed him to serve as a spiritual oncologist to a people who did have cancer, a terminal cancer, a cancer that unleashed voracious, renegade cells to eat away at their confidence in God's grace.

The prophet, like an empathetic physician, suffered with his patients as the disease consumed the Israelites' sense and soul. Driven by love for his patients, the prophet agonized over the Israelites' rejection of God's cure for their cancer. He raged against the people for hastening their spiritual demise. He groused to the LORD* about the unwinnable struggle God had called him to fight.

Jeremiah's call

Jeremiah was squeamish about serving as God's prophet. That was true from the day the LORD appointed him. He reports, "The word of the LORD came to me, saying, 'Before I formed you in the womb I knew you, before you were born I set you apart; I appointed you as a prophet to the nations'" (Jeremiah 1:4,5). Though God had chosen him from eternity for this position, Jeremiah resisted. He pleaded, "Alas, Sovereign LORD, I do not know how to speak; I am too young" (Jeremiah 1:6).

God was not put off. He understood the fear behind Jeremiah's excuses: "Do not say, 'I am too young.' You must go to everyone I send you to and say whatever I command you. Do not be afraid of them, for I am with you and will rescue you" (Jeremiah 1:7,8).

Then the LORD took an extra step to impress Jeremiah with the divine commitment that would empower the prophet's ministry: "The LORD reached out his hand and touched my mouth and said to me, 'I have put my words in your mouth'" (Jeremiah 1:9).

---

* Note: The word LORD (a translation of the Hebrew *Yahweh*) appears over six hundred times in the book of Jeremiah. That's the name God uses whenever he wants to emphasize that he is the God of full, free, faithful, and forever grace. Whenever that special name appeared, God was reminding his Old Testament believers that he would send his Son. For us it is a reminder that he did as he promised. He sent his Son to be our Savior.

On average, the word LORD (Yahweh) appears more than ten times in every chapter of Jeremiah. Amid all of God's foreboding pronouncements of punishment is evidence of the bright future. The Messiah is coming to face the full punishment for every sin and win our full forgiveness.

This book uses the capitalization of God's special name (LORD) throughout as a reminder of his love and gracious promises in all of our trials and challenges.

The Lord also provided the prophet with a mission statement: "I appoint you over nations and kingdoms to uproot and tear down, to destroy and overthrow, to build and to plant" (Jeremiah 1:10).

Jeremiah would never win a standing ovation from the people of Judah. Yes, the Spirit would use him to build and to plant (see Jeremiah 31:27-34). But the other four verbs in that mission statement foretold the upheaval his ministry would cause. Even in times of spiritual health, a prophet who uproots and tears down finds meager welcome. But Jerusalem was morally bereft. Its citizens viewed the prophet as worthy of their rejection, contempt, and opposition.

Jeremiah's role was a difficult one. God used him to call Judah to repentance one final time. For centuries, God had patiently yet pointedly worked to bring his people to spiritual health. For centuries, prophet after prophet spoke for him. For centuries, his people refused the treatment their Physician offered.

Jeremiah's ministry would not change their attitudes. He pleaded with stonyhearted people who would rather fault the Lord than respond to his warnings. The burden of his ministry often overwhelmed him.

A history of spiritual rebellion

After the deaths of King David (c. 970 b.c.) and King Solomon (c. 931 b.c.), the cords that held the 12 tribes of Israel together were shredded. Two nations resulted: Israel in the north and Judah in the south. Every king in Israel rejected the Lord. Two hundred years later (721 b.c.), as God had threatened, the land of Israel was decimated. Assyrian warriors ravaged the people. Those who survived were resettled across an empire that straddled most of the Middle East. Within two or three generations, assimilated by their new cultures, those tribes of Israel disappeared.

Twenty years later (701 b.c.), Judah barely escaped an enemy attack. Assyrian troops, numbering 185,000, bivouacked in the hills surrounding Jerusalem. Judah should have become a victim of the same fate as Israel. But God responded to King Hezekiah's prayer with a miracle. In one night, the angel of the LORD massacred the entire enemy army (2 Kings 19:35).

The LORD intended this military miracle to be a confirmation of his gracious commitment to his spiritually adulterous people. It was another appeal for them to embrace him as their God. At first, the LORD's treatment program had a positive effect. During the remainder of Hezekiah's reign (c. 715–687 B.C.), Judah's spiritual cancer showed signs of remission. Unfortunately, the cancer quickly flared again, metastasized, and became terminal.

In the slightly more than 150 years between the Assyrian destruction of Samaria and the Babylonian destruction of Jerusalem, only one of Judah's kings, besides Hezekiah, committed himself to serving the LORD. For 31 years in about the middle of that time, King Josiah (c. 640–609 B.C.) instituted spiritual reforms. But that reformation fizzled. The sins of Josiah's grandfather, Manasseh, had fatally infected Judah (2 Kings 23:19-27). A succession of morally corrupt and spiritually dead monarchs followed Josiah. Judah endorsed them until Babylon destroyed the nation in 587 B.C.

Jeremiah's place in history

Jeremiah's time of service spanned this death-spiral era. He spoke for the LORD from the middle of Josiah's reign to slightly beyond the destruction of Jerusalem (c. 626–585 B.C.). God's message through Jeremiah was "I am bringing disaster on this people, the fruit of their schemes, because they have not listened to my words and have rejected my law" (Jeremiah 6:19). The people's dedication to false gods and prophets, adultery, and lovelessness condemned them.

"My people have committed two sins," God announced. "They have forsaken me, the spring of living water, and have dug their own cisterns, broken cisterns that cannot hold water"

(Jeremiah 2:13). Judah had rejected the life-giving water of God's abundant grace. The people chose instead the sieve-like cisterns, gods created in human minds by human hands with human characteristics.

For his efforts, Jeremiah experienced ridicule and harassment. Family members betrayed him. He endured beatings and imprisonment. He lived through the famine and disease brought on by Nebuchadnezzar's siege of Jerusalem. He saw the city destroyed by raping, rampaging soldiers. He lived in the desolate aftermath of that war's horrors.

Though Jeremiah faced rejection, torture, and death threats throughout his ministry, God kept his promise. "I will make you a wall to this people, a fortified wall of bronze," he assured Jeremiah. "They will fight against you but will not overcome you, for I am with you to rescue and save you" (Jeremiah 15:20). The fact that Jeremiah survived the murderous plots of powerful people in Jerusalem, as well as the total destruction of the city, demonstrates how irrevocable God's promises are.

Jeremiah's complaints

So what does this have to do with my cancer? With yours?

> When he complained, he displayed admirable strength in his faith in God.

Jeremiah surprises me. I am surprised that he stood Atlas-like, as though the weight of the world rested on his shoulders. He clung to God's promise that he was a bronze wall that would withstand any assault. Even when he complained, he displayed admirable strength in his faith in God. He spoke truth to a corrupt society. He proclaimed God's threats to hostile ears. He shared the good news of God's love to rejecting hearts.

But Jeremiah was not the perfect prophet. He often hated his job. He threatened to quit. He filled his books with heartrending grumbling.

Imagine the prophet's agonized face when he spit out these words, "Cursed be the man who brought my father the news, who made him very glad, saying, 'A child is born to you—a son!'" (Jeremiah 20:15). Do you see his clenched fists? his angry eyes?

Jeremiah continues his tirade, "Why did I ever come out of the womb to see trouble and sorrow and to end my days in shame?" (Jeremiah 20:18).

A cancer survivor's lesson in Jeremiah

We cancer warriors find Jeremiah relatable. He offers us a true-to-life example of a Christian bewildered by unfairness, pain, and victimization. People who battle cancer can find in his struggles their struggles, in his complaints their complaints. In Jeremiah we find someone we can understand and we find our God who understands. And in God we find the ultimate and unending power to battle on.

> We cancer warriors find Jeremiah relatable. He offers us a true-to-life example of a Christian bewildered by unfairness, pain, and victimization.

"I am with you to rescue and save you" was God's commitment to Jeremiah (Jeremiah 15:20). That's also his commitment to us. We share the same Messiah as Jeremiah. Consequently, the same heaven is ours. The same adoption into God's family is ours. The same inviolable promises are ours. We know how God kept that promise to Jeremiah. He must do the same for us. Jesus' Easter victory affirms God's power and love for us as we face not only life's struggles but also death.

In the next chapters, we will consider when complaining, especially about cancer, is appropriate. We will examine factors that encourage us to complain. We will seek the Spirit's help to view those causes of complaint with eyes that stay focused on Jesus.

Stand strong. In his Son, God has also made you "a fortified wall of bronze" (Jeremiah 15:20).

Prayer

Holy LORD, the God of unbreakable promises, impress on me that your commitment to me is every bit as intense as your commitment to Jeremiah. In those times when it seems I can take no more, when the fears overwhelm, and when the burden is too heavy, speak to me through your Word. Tell me, "I will make you... a fortified wall of bronze; . . . I am with you to rescue and save you" (Jeremiah 15:20). Point me to Jesus' empty cross and tomb where your pledges to me are underwritten. Amen.

Chapter 2
WHY WE COMPLAIN

A mother with three young children wrote this on her Caring-Bridge blog.

> I will be blunt. I can't handle hearing, even one more time, "So nice," or "So great," or "You're so lucky," or "So glad you didn't have to have chemo or radiation."
>
> Let me just say, I know this. Though I was ready to do both [chemo and radiation], if that is how I was so directed. But, yes, my cancer graciously didn't warrant it, as it was small in size.
>
> Let me tell you right now, every time I hear this I actually hear, "Your cancer was virtually nothing, so get over it, move on," and "Who gives a rip?" I know they may not mean this at all, but this is *most* definitely how the receiver of such words who is in my shoes will take it.
>
> This is how I would have really liked to respond—and I would love to use a super sarcastic, sassy voice (so if you read it like that you'll get the full effect ;-)).
>
> You are so right. My cancer was nothing. Here's the proof:
>
> The fact that I had two years without a solid diagnosis though I had bleeding, pain, stinging, tingling, shooting pain, and discomfort in my nipple and endless bras that would be ruined due to salves I would try and that would end up being stained with blood is absolutely nothing.

The fact that I had to go through three different painful biopsies to figure out what cancer treatment I needed was nothing.

The fact that I had a lumpectomy thinking that was all I would need along with radiation, which turned out to be wrong was nothing.

The fact that I then had to have a mastectomy was nothing.

The fact that I have a terrible time with nausea for weeks after each and every surgery due to major issues with anesthesia is nothing.

The fact that I haven't felt like myself since before this all started means nil.

The fact that I had fake implants inserted into me to try to make me feel semi-normal, but, quite honestly, they make you feel super odd, uncomfortable, and sore means *nothing*.

The fact that one of my breasts is off the charts swollen (at least that is how it feels) and I'm not sure if it will go down anytime soon is totally no big deal.

The fact that amidst all these surgeries and tests, I had to parent three children, one of whom is special needs is NADA. (Laura Bublitz, https://www.caringbridge.org)

Christians will never complain. Right?

The Christian woman who wrote these paragraphs demonstrates that believers do complain sometimes. Bitterly. Angrily. Sarcastically.

Complaining believers

This is not news: The Scriptures contain numerous examples of complaining believers.

At the top of that list is the frequent whining of the wilderness-wandering Israelites. For four decades God's people complained about Moses, Aaron, and the LORD.

Numbers 21:4-6 provides an example: "The people grew impatient on the way; they spoke against God and against Moses, and said, 'Why have you brought us up out of Egypt to die in the wilderness? There is no bread! There is no water! And we detest this miserable food!' Then the LORD sent venomous snakes among them; they bit the people and many Israelites died."

> The Scriptures contain numerous examples of complaining believers.

We can even add Moses to that list of complainers. After the people complained about their food, the LORD was angry and Moses was troubled. He turned to the LORD with his complaint: "Why have you brought this trouble on your servant? What have I done to displease you that you put the burden of all these people on me? If this is how you are going to treat me, please go ahead and kill me" (Numbers 11:11,15). He also complained about the Israelites (I can't blame him) when he struck the rock at Meribah to produce water for them. "Listen, you rebels," he scolded, "must we bring you water out of this rock?" (Numbers 20:10). He was so upset with the Israelites that he neglected to credit God for the miracle of supplying water from the rock. The consequence: He forfeited his opportunity to set foot in the Promised Land (Numbers 20:12).

Abraham was not happy that the LORD took so long in keeping his promise to give him a son. "Sovereign LORD, what can you give me since I remain childless?" he whined (Genesis 15:2).

Asaph, a writer of some of the psalms, wrote, "I envied the arrogant when I saw the prosperity of the wicked. They have no struggles; their bodies are healthy and strong. Surely in vain I have kept my heart pure and have washed my hands in innocence" (Psalm 73:3,4,13).

Solomon also grumbled about that same supposed unfairness, "There is something else meaningless that occurs on earth: the righteous who get what the wicked deserve, and the wicked who get what the righteous deserve" (Ecclesiastes 8:14).

Reasons not to complain

Of course, there is an incontestable reason for Christians to refuse to gripe: our adoption into God's eternal family through Jesus. Paul urges, "Do everything without grumbling or arguing, so that you may become blameless and pure, 'children of God without fault in a warped and crooked generation.' Then you will shine among them like stars in the sky" (Philippians 2:14,15).

Another reason is the threat of punishment that comes with violating God's proscription against our clucking about his leadership. First Corinthians 10:10 warns, "Do not grumble, as some of [the Israelites in the wilderness] did—and were killed by the destroying angel." James 5:9 counsels, "Don't grumble against one another, brothers and sisters, or you will be judged. The Judge is standing at the door!"

> Jeremiah complained. A lot. His frequent grousing gained him the reputation as the "weeping prophet."

The bottom line: Grumbling about the challenges we face in life is not appropriate. Especially for those who have found rest in God's grace.

A prophet's complaints

But . . . Jeremiah complained. A lot. His frequent grousing gained him the reputation as the "weeping prophet." Jeremiah even describes himself that way: "Oh, that my head were a spring of water and my eyes a fountain of tears! I would weep day and night for the slain of my people" (Jeremiah 9:1).

Jeremiah complained that he had been faithful to the LORD, but the LORD had not been faithful to him (Jeremiah 15:16-18). He complained that Judah responded to his ministry by digging a pit for him (Jeremiah 18:19,20). He even found fault with the LORD for deceiving him into preaching God's Word (Jeremiah 20:7,8).

In Luther's *Preface to the Prophet Jeremiah,* the Reformer says, "He was a sad and troubled prophet and lived in miserably evil days. Besides he had a peculiarly difficult ministry. For over forty years, down to the captivity, he had to say hard things to obstinately wicked people. Still it did little good. He had to look on while the people went from bad to worse, always wanting to kill him, and putting him to much hardship" (Martin Luther, *Luther's Works.* Edited by Jaroslav Pelikan and Helmut T. Lehmann. American Edition. Vol. 35. St. Louis: Concordia Publishing House; Philadelphia: Fortress Press, 1955–1986, p. 280).

Did Jeremiah's dire, dangerous situation justify his complaining? There's a bigger question: Is complaining ever justified? Dare we complain about anything, including our battle with cancer? Let's first examine some of the reasons we choose to complain.

Why do we complain?

Life's traumas provide fertile ground for complaints to easily germinate. In the book of Lamentations, Jeremiah wrestled with those weeds. In these chapters, the prophet decries the horrors that scarred his ruined city.

The year was 721 B.C. Babylon had made an example of Jerusalem. Its message to neighboring cities under its boot was clear: Don't let this happen to you. Submission is better than rebellion.

After starving the city into submission, Nebuchadnezzar's troops rampaged through Jerusalem. They murdered on a whim, looted whatever sparkled in their eyes, and committed war's worst atrocities. Thousands lay dead among the ruins. Thousands more, driven like cattle, marched away to distant lands and a fearsome future.

Jeremiah and the thousands who were left among the toppled, smoldering buildings stumbled on. They survived the terror. They would never recover. They were crippled by what they had experienced. Some imploded: scarred, staggered, shattered. Others, zombie-like, shuffled from one putrefied day to the next. PTSD is not a modern phenomenon. The city's devastation crushed all hope. The stench of smoke and death appeared to outshout every prayer for help.

Think of Manhattan the day those airliners brought down the Twin Towers. Think beyond the rubble, the ash, and the bodies. Think of the twisted wreckage of the lives that were seared by the heat of the flames and were choked by the storms of dust. Think of the trauma endured by the people who survived when friends and office mates did not. Now consider surviving the annihilation not of city blocks but of an entire city.

Like maggots in August garbage, countless reasons for complaint bred in the dung heap that Jerusalem had become. They are the same reasons that encourage people with cancer to complain.

1. We complain because we are not in control.

We complain when the situation seems hopeless. When our circumstances seem beyond our control. When we believe we are victims.

After surveying the aftermath of the bedlam that Babylon had inflicted on Jerusalem, Jeremiah complained. The LORD's spokesperson spoke to God first in faith and then in frustration: "You, LORD, reign forever; your throne endures from generation to generation. Why do you always forget us? Why do you forsake us so long?" (Lamentations 5:19,20).

Walking through the rubble of the city, the prophet realized that there was nothing he could do to save his home. Over the decades of his ministry, he stood as the bronze wall that God predicted he would be (Jeremiah 1:18). He proclaimed the

LORD's powerful Word. But the people of Jerusalem plugged their ears. Now God had carried out his threat. Convinced he and his people were abandoned, Jeremiah wailed, "Why do you forsake us?"

Were your emotions similar when you learned you had cancer? Or when the chemo began to exact a toll on your body, robbing you of strength, mental agility, and will? Or when your oncologist informed you that in spite of your sacrifices, the cancer was now terminal?

> The Spirit has much to teach us about learning to trust the choices our Father makes for our lives.

Nothing could undo the carnage that lay in the streets of Jerusalem. Though the prophet did everything God had told him to do, he was not able to change the outcome the LORD had threatened. The Almighty said this would happen: "These people have stubborn and rebellious hearts; they have turned aside and gone away. Should I not punish them for this? . . . Should I not avenge myself on such a nation as this?" (Jeremiah 5:23,29). God's warnings had become reality. The current situation and the future beyond lay outside of Jeremiah's power and control.

Your cancer is beyond your power and control too. The eventual outcome of your disease does not rest in your hands. Or your doctors' hands. No little frustration—and trepidation—attaches to that realization.

You understand Jeremiah's yowling: "Restore us to yourself, LORD, that we may return; renew our days as of old unless you have utterly rejected us and are angry with us beyond measure" (Lamentations 5:21,22).

The Spirit has much to teach us about learning to trust the choices our Father makes for our lives. We'll get to those instructions. For now, let's move on to another reason we complain.

2. We complain because we anticipate a negative outcome.

Deepak Chopra wrote, "The best use of imagination is creativity; the worst use of imagination is anxiety." I agree with few of Chopra's views, but he is correct about the worst use of imagination. Consider the way Jeremiah envisioned his situation in Lamentations chapter 4.

The magnificent buildings of Jerusalem, including the LORD's temple, were rubble. Jeremiah must have thought, "It is impossible for my people ever to recover from such destruction."

In despair, Jeremiah mourned, "The punishment of my people is greater than that of Sodom, which was overthrown in a moment without a hand turned to help her. The LORD has given full vent to his wrath; he has poured out his fierce anger. He kindled a fire in Zion that consumed her foundations" (Lamentations 4:6,11).

Cancer unleashes millions of cells that act like fanatic suicide squads. The daunting odds against the defeat of these armed extremists loom large in our minds. Our demise seems inevitable. Complaint about our situation comes without difficulty.

Radiation therapy and chemotherapy have a cumulative effect. Their impact grows the longer the therapy continues. Worry is similar, yet it never brings healing.

When I graduated from the seminary in 1975, I was assigned to a new congregation on the Gulf of Mexico about 100 miles south of Tampa, Florida. Less than 300 miles south of there was Havana, Cuba.

My wife and I never considered Cuba to be a threat to our safety. But my wife's 80-year-old grandfather believed that Fidel Castro was on the verge of invading the United States. It started with a nightmare that he believed to be a prophecy. He convinced himself that Cuban armies would land at Key West and make their way north through the Florida peninsula. No amount of information or appeal to logic could change his mind. Yes, he knew next to nothing about Cuba or life in Florida. Yes, he had never journeyed far from his central Wisconsin home. And yet he said, "Don't confuse me with facts. I've made up my mind. You are in grave danger."

Grandpa didn't worry about just us. He spent large portions of each day fretting about the terrible things that could happen to his loved ones. His worries had a cumulative effect: The more he worried, the more his worries increased. What started as "There's an infinitesimal chance that Cuba could invade Florida" over time became "Cuban armies are sailing toward Florida; their primary objective is capturing my grandchildren and great-grandchildren."

Cumulative worry about negative cancer outcomes results in cascading complaints. When worry takes over in our minds, a cancer diagnosis morphs into a death sentence. And this grows in spite of the fact that many cancers can be cured and many others slowed to a crawl. When worry takes over, no amount of reason can unseat it. We anticipate the worst and cannot imagine an alternative outcome. Complaint seems reasonable.

Here's an example: Consider the jumps in logic that caused David to exaggerate in Psalm 12:1-4: "Help, LORD, for no one is faithful anymore; those who are loyal have vanished from the human race. Everyone lies to their neighbor; they flatter with their lips but harbor deception in their hearts. May the LORD silence all flattering lips and every boastful tongue—those who say, 'By our tongues we will prevail; our own lips will defend us—who is lord over us?'"

> When we allow ourselves to worry about possible negative outcomes, we complain.

David sees things at their worst. Yet he does regain his spiritual balance by the end of the psalm. He pledges to trust God's Word rather than his emotions: "The words of the LORD are flawless, like silver purified in a crucible, like gold refined seven times. You, LORD, will keep the needy safe and will protect us forever from the wicked, who freely strut about when what is vile is honored by the human race" (Psalm 12:6-8).

Like David, when we allow ourselves to worry about possible negative outcomes, we complain. There's a solution to complaints that have run amok. David found it.

3. We complain because we are going through something we have never experienced before.

I think it's endearing when my five-year-old grandchildren complain because addition and subtraction are challenging to them. I mastered 2 plus 2 equals 4 many decades ago. But for my kindergarten-aged grandkids, math is an unexplored jungle. It's daunting. Difficult. Ominous.

> Cancer treatments, medical jargon, hospital routines and rules, medications, and doctor visits mangle what used to be our normal.

Every fresh challenge in life is similar. Who is not intimidated by starting a new job, developing a new relationship, learning a new skill? Confronting cancer is no different.

Jeremiah had no experience with the jungle that surrounded him after Jerusalem fell to the Babylonians. Many of the assumptions that guided him before now malfunctioned. He laments, "Remember, LORD, what has happened to us; look, and see our disgrace. Our inheritance has been turned over to strangers, our homes to foreigners. Our ancestors sinned and are no more, and we bear their punishment. Slaves rule over us, and there is no one to free us from their hands" (Lamentations 5:1,2,7,8).

You can probably understand Jeremiah's muddle. Cancer treatments, medical jargon, hospital routines and rules, medications, and doctor visits mangle what used to be our normal. Like Alice, we discover ourselves in a topsy-turvy Wonderland haunted by Mad Hatters and Cheshire Cats. In this absurd universe, we yearn for the predictability of our former life. But regaining our former life is impossible, and that makes matters worse.

A man with cancer told me, "My therapist always says, 'This was the old you and where you were.'" He lifted his right hand palm up to demonstrate where he was. "'What you are going through sucks right now,' he tells me, 'but this is where you are going to.'" He held his left palm higher than his right. "'You will be a better person. Think about all the ways you can help people when you get through this.'"

Think of all the ways you'll help people. A wonderful thought—but it's next to impossible. No, it is impossible to envision a brighter, more beautiful future when the present we know is ripped away. Cancer brings us into unchartered territory. Whoever we were BC (before cancer) disappears. A new person, a brave explorer designed for pathless wilderness, needs to emerge. That transition involves a struggle. It requires a reframing of the way we perceive ourselves and, often, of the way we perceive our God.

> Cancer brings us into unchartered territory.

Usually, the first step in becoming this brave explorer is overcoming the "There ain't no way this can be happening to me" denial.

A breast cancer survivor told me, "My high school friend brought me a prayer quilt before I started chemo. It was very special because she was in the group that made the quilt. And I really liked it. Yet there was this realization: I need a cancer quilt. I'm a cancer person."

She continued, "The thing I hate about going to the doctor's office is seeing the people whose cancer is much worse. I tell myself, I am not one of them. But the strange thing is, I tell myself that even though I did the whole thing: surgery, chemo. Even though

I completely lost my hair and I wore head wraps. You don't want to be in that group."

In the battle against cancer, we are like the grade school children who are picked for the unpopular softball team. Our teammates are not the kids we would have chosen to hang around with. In our group, there are no stars. Everyone is trying to figure out how to play the game. Our team has no one proficient; everyone is struggling to swing the bat and catch the ball. How disorienting, not to mention disheartening, to admit that we belong on this team.

That is the reason our denial of our situation appears attractive. We don't want to be in this group so we deny and then complain.

Cancer bewilders—death threats will do that. But for Christians, cancer also promises never-before-experienced benefits. My friend's therapist was right: We can become better people because of cancer. God's grace guarantees it.

4. We complain because we are afraid.

The scorched remains of Jerusalem became the grave for Jeremiah's sense of confidence. Many of the constants that created security in his life were gone along with Jerusalem's population.

After the Babylonian army marched off toward additional conquests elsewhere, the seeds of fear sprang to life. Fear thrived among the rubble. Like an invasive weed, it choked out any thought of peace or positive future. Jeremiah and the others left behind protested, "How will we live? Where will we live? What kind of life will we live?"

> The greatest losses in life generate fear.

The greatest losses in life generate fear. Lose your job; gain fear of your future. Lose a loved one; find anguish and worry as unwelcomed friends. Lose your health; discover dread has filled the vacuum.

The prophet described his fright when he moaned, "I am the man who has seen affliction by the rod of the LORD's wrath. He has filled me with bitter herbs and given me gall to drink. He has broken my teeth with gravel; he has trampled me in the dust. I have been deprived of peace; I have forgotten what prosperity is" (Lamentations 3:1,15-17).

How many of your complaints about cancer trace their genesis to fear? Do you fear that no cure exists? that your treatment protocol will fail? that not even a stalemate is possible? Is your fear that the pain will be unbearable, the loss unacceptable, or the mightiest of effort unfruitful? Complaint springs from such fears.

A friend told me, "One of the things about having cancer that scares me most is being told there is nothing more to be done. I wonder what it would be like to be sitting in that little room and the doctor basically says, 'We've done everything we can.' That moment scares me more than anything."

"Why does that frighten you?" I asked.

"Because, at that point, I will be helpless. Up until now, everyone has been telling me, you gotta keep hope alive. But then, when the doctor tells me the cancer is terminal, all that is taken away. All the hope will be gone. It scares me. Sometimes I have dreams about it, how it will all go down."

5. We complain because we are uncomfortable in our present situation.

In the late 1970s, my mother was hospitalized because of a kidney stone she could not pass. Her doctors fought to ease her agony but with no appreciable success. She was in her 40s. She had high school-aged children. She had so many reasons to live. But I remember her calling out, "Lord, please take this pain away. Please, Father, give me relief. Or just let me die. I can't take this anymore. Please, God! Just let me die!"

Jeremiah's situation was even more wretched. His pain surpassed the physical. It erupted from his soul in a bubbling flow of molten emotion. His protest exploded from a heart-shaped caldera that was dark and dread-filled.

> I am the man who has seen affliction by the rod of the LORD's wrath. He has driven me away and made me walk in darkness rather than light. He has besieged me and surrounded me with bitterness and hardship. Even when I call out or cry for help, he shuts out my prayer. I became the laughingstock of all my people; they mock me in song all day long. So I say, "My splendor is gone and all that I had hoped from the LORD." I remember my affliction and my wandering, the bitterness and the gall. I well remember them, and my soul is downcast within me. (Lamentations 3:1,2,5,8,14,18-20)

Have you complained that your splendor is gone and with it all you had hoped the LORD would do for you? The Hebrew word translated as "splendor" can mean "something good which lasts." It's the bright things that give us confidence and make us complete. Consequently, this word meaning "splendor" can refer to something that will perpetually endure. It is something that is always dependable. Jeremiah moans because his splendor—his self-worth and confidence—was gone.

> Cancer can bring us to feel Jeremiah's lack of comfort. It can rob us of the assurance that life has a foundation no earthquake can shake, a confidence no storm clouds can obscure.

Cancer can bring us to feel Jeremiah's lack of comfort. It can rob us of the assurance that life has a foundation no earthquake can shake, a confidence no storm clouds can obscure. When cancer deprives us of our physical well-being, it hacks away at the roots of a source of our security. We may feel that if we can't depend on our body to protect and care for us, what is there? Then flailed by frustration, we complain.

When I was growing up, my family had a dachshund named Schnappsie. Late in life he developed chronic back problems. Whenever he suffered through an episode with his spine, he refused to be held or even touched. This family pet, who normally was happy being a lapdog, snarled and snipped at the slightest attempt at contact.

Humans in pain are no different. Humans suffering from cancer—its pain or its threats—can be more truculent than Schnappsie ever was. What are the ways your lack of comfort causes you to complain?

6. We complain because we feel we don't deserve what we are going through.

Jeremiah convulsed over the *unjustified* horror his devastated city suffered at the hands of the Babylonian army. He judged that the pillaging, predation, and pestilence had far outstripped the godlessness that had slithered there. God's punishment, he argued, did not fit Jerusalem's crime.

"Look, LORD," he demands, "and consider: Whom have you ever treated like this? Should women eat their offspring, the children they have cared for? Should priest and prophet be killed in the sanctuary of the Lord? Young and old lie together in the dust of the streets; my young men and young women have fallen by the sword. You have slain them in the day of your anger; you have slaughtered them without pity" (Lamentations 2:20,21).

"That's not fair!" my grandkids bellyache when they perceive someone has gotten a bigger cookie. But it's not only grade school-aged children who complain about unfairness.

Cancer, along with its tortures of heart and body, screams discrimination. Cancer twists "Why me?" into more of an indictment than a question. Cancer, we insist, should be reserved to punish the wickedest of the wicked. God should not bring this calamity on good people, on his people, on me.

> Cancer twists "Why me?" into more of an indictment than a question.

Have you ever said—or at least felt—"It's not fair that cancer eats away at me! Lord, you are slaughtering me without pity"?

"I have that 'why me?' discussion with God quite often," a man I interviewed told me. "There have been nights where I have literally cried out at the sky, 'Why is this happening to me?' Usually it's not the cancer but something else that puts me over the edge, some other problem that makes me complain about the unfairness. I tell God, 'LORD, don't I have enough on my plate already? Come on, give me a break. I can't do all these things.'"

He offered an example: "Being around healthy people gets me to think about how unfair my cancer is. For example, we might go for a walk. I can walk for 20 minutes, up to a half hour. I used to run for miles. But now I'll see a couple run by and I'll think, 'That could be my wife and me.' That gets me every time."

7. We complain because God has violated our plans for our lives.

Cancer is life-shattering.

Many find that their life goals are monstrously morphed after a cancer diagnosis. Like Humpty Dumpty, their plans shatter so badly that not even the king's horses and king's men are able to put them back together again. Cancer demands that an unsought, unpalatable future emerges from the eggshells lying amidst the goo splattered on the ground.

Sloshing through the broken eggshells of his life plans, Jeremiah understood that the future he had envisioned for his people and himself would never happen. "Look, LORD, and consider, for I am despised," he gripes. "Is it nothing to you, all you who pass by? Look around and see. Is any suffering like my suffering that was inflicted on me, that the LORD brought on me in the day of his fierce anger? . . . He made me desolate, faint all the day long" (Lamentations 1:11-13).

I came home from my prostatectomy wearing a catheter. During the day it was tethered to my leg. At night it hung from the side of the bed. I felt humiliated. A 60-year-old man who had no control over his bladder! After two weeks the catheter was removed, but the urinary incontinence hung around. Adult diapers and pads became part of my wardrobe for weeks.

> Cancer sidetracks— if not derails— the goals we had for our lives.

One day my mother asked how my recovery was progressing. I sighed and admitted that I had wet the bed the night before. I hadn't done that for six decades. "Jim, you wet the bed?! Shame on you," she said, pretending she was a mother to a four-year-old. In fairness, Mom was trying to bring some humor to the situation. I did not hear it that way.

My plans for being a 60-something adult never included incontinence. Not even incontinence that would eventually fade and disappear. I was miserable.

Cancer can bring much more severe hardships than the embarrassment of incontinence. In fact, the medical issues you have faced probably should make me embarrassed even to mention the inconvenience of incontinence I faced.

But the point of these paragraphs is not to gauge which of us suffers more from cancer and its treatment. The point is that cancer sidetracks—if not derails—the goals we had for our lives.

How easy to complain with the prophet, "Is any suffering like my suffering that was inflicted on me, that the LORD brought on me in the day of his fierce anger? . . . He made me desolate, faint all the day long" (Lamentations 1:12,13).

Cancer provides ample reason for us to feel justified about complaining. However, is complaining ever justified? Does it ever serve a wholesome purpose? Is God ever pleased when we complain? Let's examine those questions in the next chapter.

Prayer

Loving Father, I can find many reasons to justify my complaints. Thank you for helping me think about the ways I justify my grumbling. Help me evaluate my reasons for grousing about my cancer. Make me willing to admit my failure to trust you. Remind me that you will never desert me and that your love for me offers forgiveness that covers all my sin and provides fortitude for my future. Keep the assurances of Jesus' resurrection as the focus of my life. Amen.

Chapter 3
THE BENEFITS OF COMPLAINING

Cancer offers us convincing reasons to sing the dirges of Lamentations along with Jeremiah.

But does harmonizing with Jeremiah provide any benefit? Is God ever pleased by our complaining? Is the lesson just to know that someone like Jeremiah also complained? Is there something else we can learn from the prophet?

Let's think about our complaining again. Complaining is a normal human experience whenever the page turns in our lives. We have grown familiar with the past and expect the next page to be just like the others. But often when we begin reading that next page, it is not like the others. We complain!

Complaining can be the language of searching. We don't like the new page. We search for answers and something different, especially when it is impossible to turn back the difficult page and move on. That's where Jeremiah was. He could not go back. He searched for answers to a different and frightening new life. That's where we often find ourselves too.

> Complaining can be the language of searching.

Our complaints express the values we allow to guide us. They identify the lies we have grown comfortable with and that fuel our chaotic emotions and skewed perceptions. Once we analyze our complaints, the fog dissipates and the truth of our situation snaps into focus.

But be warned: If our goal in complaining is just to complain, our search will be frustrated. Venting our frustrations may seem satisfying, but it produces no resolution.

Here's an example. A married couple came to me for counseling. The husband recognized he had allowed competing priorities— particularly his golf game—to erode his relationship with his wife. He wanted to begin again. He wanted to make their marriage stronger. The wife, though, only seemed interested in rehashing all the ways he had failed her. In each session, she referred to a notebook in which she kept a detailed record of his every infraction.

This woman was unmoved by her husband's apologies. She was indifferent to listening to anything the Bible had to say about forgiving her husband and rebuilding their marriage. She refused to move beyond complaining about her husband's shortcomings. You won't be surprised to learn that their marriage ended in divorce.

> Complaining never changes our situation. Complaining only indicates that the situation requires healing.

Complaining never changes our situation. Complaining only indicates that the situation requires healing. Complaining is the signal we need to find healing in the love and empowerment God provides in his Word.

Jeremiah complains, but he does not stop there. What can we learn from him and his complaining?

1. Complaining surfaces the lie.

At the heart of our complaints are lies. Exaggerations. Problem magnification. Fact fabrication. Disinformation.

Behind every one of the reasons we complain stands a lie. When we complain because we are not in control, the lie is that we can

THE BENEFITS OF COMPLAINING

be in control. When we complain in anticipation of a negative outcome, the lie is that our Savior will renege on his promise to shepherd us through the shadowy valleys to green pastures, banquet tables, and his home. When we complain because a new experience has disoriented us, the lie is that our all-knowing God is also flummoxed. When we complain because we are afraid, the lie is that the all-powerful LORD will not come to our rescue.

Our complaints bring those lies into the light of truth. There they can be identified, repented of, and rejected. Complaining can be helpful when it drives into the open the lies that fuel our vitriol. There we can evaluate their deceptions.

We miss that benefit when we allow our complaints to fester inside. Sometimes we Christians imagine that God will reject us if we give voice to our bitterness. The truth is that we can't hide our anguish from him. We might as well openly talk it over with him.

A troubled David provides us with an example. In Psalm 38, he mourned under the weight of his guilt: "I am feeble and utterly crushed; I groan in anguish of heart." Nonetheless, he was willing to bring his burden to his God. The reason? The LORD's omniscience. "All my longings lie open before you, Lord; my sighing is not hidden from you" (verses 8,9).

Certainly, the infinitely wise and powerful LORD understands the stress that we labor under. Psalm 147:5 explains, "Great is our Lord and mighty in power; his understanding has no limits." Psalm 103:14 adds, "He knows how we are formed, he remembers that we are dust."

2. Talk through those lies with your Father and others.

Talk with your Father about the things that trouble you, Peter urges. "Cast all your anxiety on him because he cares for you" (1 Peter 5:7). How much does he care for you? "This is how God showed his love among us: He sent his one and only Son into the world that we might live through him" (1 John 4:9).

Complaints spring from a view of life that has warped assurances of God's love for us. The new page of life is different, and our first reaction may be to think that our Father has abandoned us. We overcome those complaints first by explaining to God what we are seeing. The next step is more critical. We listen to the Spirit describe what we should be seeing. Time in his Word, where we listen to the Spirit's voice, is essential to moving beyond our grumbling and complaining.

We hear God speaking to us whenever we are in contact with the Bible. Sometimes that contact with the Scriptures comes to us through mature Christians. Brothers and sisters in Jesus can help us find our way through the deception behind our complaints. They can provide additional voices through which the Spirit will challenge the lies and replace them with his truth. Talk about your frustrations with seasoned, veteran believers. Seek their advice. Ask for their prayers.

Recognize, however, that not every mature Christian will work as a sounding board. One of the people I interviewed for this book is a cancer survivor who has supported friends during their cancer battles. "I bared my soul to one of my sisters during my cancer treatments. I wasn't as open with my other sister. I came to understand that the person with whom I needed to share my complaints and concerns and fears had to be someone who would 'hear' me, who would understand my heart, not just my words. That person had to be someone whose reaction to whatever I said I could trust."

Before choosing a treatment plan for my prostate cancer, I weighed "watchful waiting" against surgery, radiation, and less researched treatments. Of the options, only watchful waiting did not threaten the side effects of incontinence and erectile dysfunction (ED). The downside of watchful waiting was that the cancer would continue to spread. That could require more aggressive cancer treatments later on.

At first, I kept my deliberations to myself. I found it difficult to bring up incontinence and ED in a conversation with family or friends. Eventually, I shared my concerns with my wife.

"You do as you please," she said. "But I want you in my life for years to come. And I want you there for our daughters. And for our grandchildren. If the side effects happen, we'll deal with them. Our Savior will see us through."

The mountain-sized problem I had made from a molehill shrunk to appropriate height. Talking through my complaint brought light to the lie that wearing protective underwear for incontinence or the inability to perform sexually would make me less of a man.

The Spirit has placed believers into our lives to help us deal with cancer's upheaval. Think especially of the mature Christians you know. You'll no doubt find them among your family and in your church. They may include the pastor God has provided to shepherd you through life. Don't settle for anyone who does not have a close relationship with Jesus. That would be like neglecting a board-certified physician to fix your broken arm in favor of a friend who has a partial box of adhesive bandages.

> The Spirit has placed believers into our lives to help us deal with cancer's upheaval.

Jeremiah was that resource to his friend and scribe Baruch. Before Jerusalem fell to Nebuchadnezzar, Baruch complained, "Woe to me! The LORD has added sorrow to my pain; I am worn out with groaning and find no rest." Jeremiah reminded Baruch about the LORD's promise: "I will bring disaster on all people, . . . but wherever you go I will let you escape with your life" (Jeremiah 45:3,5).

Does it seem strange that Jeremiah, the great complainer, was the one God used to help Baruch? It shouldn't. Who better to help us address our grumbling than someone God has brought through distress? Who better than someone who has recognized the lies of his own grousing? Who better than someone who has found hope in the truth of God's grace?

Our Father's voice chases away the complaints and welcomes us into his arms. In this Word we are reminded, "Because of the LORD's great love we are not consumed, for his compassions never fail" (Lamentations 3:22).

One more thought about the believers the Spirit has prepared to bring help to his people: God has positioned you to be a resource to another cancer warrior. He allows hardships to train you to care for others. Second Corinthians 1:4 applies to this thought: "[God] comforts us in all our troubles, so that we can comfort those in any trouble with the comfort we ourselves receive from God." Whom might you comfort?

3. Complaining drives us to find comfort in the Scriptures' assurances.

What drives your teeth-gnashing? Lack of comfort with your circumstances? Frustration because you feel you don't deserve what you are going through? Annoyance with God because he has apparently violated your life plans? God intends that these issues should drive you more deeply into his Word.

When our empty stomachs growl, it's a call to eat. When we hear the growls of our complaints, it's a signal we need more spiritual food. Complaining does not fill that need any more than belly-aching about how hungry we are fills our stomachs with supper. Complaints are just searching for some way to fill our spiritual stomachs.

"I'm hungee," one of my grandsons says when he's running on empty. The problem for anyone in the vicinity is that he isn't satisfied to say it once. His hammering howl pounds against any resistance to satisfying his hunger. He accents his chant with an agonized expression, copious tears, and rising volume.

"I hear you," his mother says calmly. "But you know that throwing a tantrum won't get you any food. What do I always tell you that you need to do?"

"But I'm hungee!" he insists, punctuating his statement with a foot stomp.

Mom remains calm. "What do you need to do?"

He sighs. Slowly. A deep breath in and then out while he composes himself. "I need to ask politely and to say please."

Whining because cancer has come to us won't produce a cure. But if we listen to the Scriptures in the midst of our complaining, we will hear our Father ask, "What do I always tell you that you need to do?" The answer: "You tell me to pay attention to what you have told me, heavenly Father. I need to pay attention to your Word."

> "You tell me to pay attention to what you have told me, heavenly Father. I need to pay attention to your Word."

Jeremiah is a good example. In Lamentations chapter 3, we see how Jeremiah relied on that answer to deal with his complaints. He begins the chapter by moaning, "I am the man who has seen affliction by the rod of the LORD's wrath." Next come 19 verses filled with examples of how God has afflicted him.

Then Jeremiah pauses. With a relaxed breath, he recalls what the LORD promised him: "Yet this I call to mind and therefore I have hope: Because of the LORD's great love we are not consumed, for his compassions never fail. They are new every morning; great is your faithfulness. I say to myself, 'The LORD is my portion; therefore I will wait for him'" (Lamentations 3:21-24).

This verse calls to mind what the Spirit had revealed to Jeremiah in much of the Old Testament. Four hundred years before, David wrote about God's "unfailing love" and how God would have mercy on him "according to [his] great compassion" (Psalm 51:1). "Your compassion, LORD, is great" (Psalm 119:156). The Scriptures taught him about God's faithfulness. "Your love, LORD, reaches to the heavens, your faithfulness to the skies" (Psalm 36:5). The Spirit has testified to Jeremiah, David, and us about God's great and enduring love and compassion. The LORD has another page for you to read—a page of his promises.

Are you complaining because you are *hungee*? Then listen to the voice of the Spirit who speaks to you in the Scriptures. Satisfy your hunger pangs on the banquet of grace he has set for you there.

Paul says of the Bible, "Everything that was written in the past was written to teach us, so that through the endurance taught in the Scriptures and the encouragement they provide we might have hope" (Romans 15:4).

> The more we study his Word, the more we are assured "that in all things God works for the good of those who love him" (Romans 8:28).

The more we study his Word, the more we are assured "that in all things God works for the good of those who love him" (Romans 8:28). The reason for that assurance? God's commitment to us in his Son. "I am convinced," Paul writes, "that neither death nor life, neither angels nor demons, neither the present nor the future, nor any powers, neither height nor depth, nor anything else in all creation, will be able to separate us from the love of God that is in Christ Jesus our Lord" (Romans 8:38,39).

While driving to and from chemotherapy, I usually listened to the Psalms on CD. My Father's gracious voice calmed me, refocused my thinking, and replaced my thoughts of whining with thoughts of winning. "Be still, and know that I am God," he would say. "I will be exalted among the nations, I will be exalted in the earth." How could I complain? Rather, I sang with the sons of Korah, "The LORD Almighty is with us; the God of Jacob is our fortress" (Psalm 46:10,11).

Through the first part of my cancer journey, I dealt with the emotional upheaval of the disease's threats and uncertainties by ignoring them. "So I have cancer," I told myself. "That's not a big deal. It's only prostate cancer. I'll get through this."

I researched the best treatment programs. I got a second opinion. I interviewed several prostate cancer survivors. I discussed the treatment plans with my wife. Based on my investigation, I made the decision to have the prostate removed. I did it all on a cerebral level. I resisted dealing with the emotions. I avoided asking myself how I felt about having cancer.

Fortunately, God did not allow me to skip his lesson. I had been missing a significant part of the journey he set as my itinerary.

I was doing the same thing that my young daughters did on our cross-country vacations. Outside their car windows, the sight of mountains and valleys, cornfields and cows, cities and towns were ready to delight. But my daughters were more interested in books, games, and, sometimes, arguing with each other. They allowed themselves to miss a valuable part of the journey.

Listen to yourself when you complain. Then meditate on your Father's Word. The Spirit will force the lies that drive your complaints into the light. Then acknowledge the lies, repent of them, and claim Jesus' forgiveness.

4. Benefitting from the journey.

God used my cancer to focus my attention on issues of the heart rather than of the head.

Up until cancer, "Suck it up and keep moving" was my mantra. I told myself, "It doesn't make any difference how you feel about your setbacks. The important thing is what you are going to do about it."

I convinced myself that real men don't complain. Real men keep putting one foot in front of the other and trudge on. Even more convincing was that pastors don't complain. They don their robes of Pollyanna piety and keep smiling. And godly husbands and fathers don't complain. They feign strength and control no matter how weak they are and how maniacal life becomes.

But life challenges that conviction. It works for a time, but I've found that allowing myself to take an honest look at my frustrations and fears instead of locking them away is a much healthier approach to life's unfairness. I've learned that surfacing how disheartened I feel about events and people—and even God—is beneficial. The internal pressures that build up because I am an imperfect person living in an imperfect world need an outlet. Complaining can serve as a relief valve. When done in an effective way, it provides relief, avoids explosion, and sets the stage for a productive way forward. Complaining not only helps us identify the lie behind it, but it also leads us to pinpoint the cause of annoyance, hurt, or fear. From there, the way is clear to seek a solution.

Severe neck pain manhandled a friend of mine. At first, he took the typical male approach: He refused to give in to the pain. When the pain knocked him to the ground, he hobbled into his doctor's office. The doctor could have prescribed medication to dull the pain. That would have relieved the symptoms, but the painkillers would have done nothing to treat the problem. The doctor ordered tests: blood tests, an MRI, X-rays, biopsies. The result: The doctor discovered that my friend had cancer. Within days the doctor launched an aggressive treatment plan.

Complaining urges us toward a diagnosis of our problem and then to a treatment plan. It has the potential to do more than help us understand the reason for our troubles. It can lead us to seek a solution. This search is important since we often complain and believe that our situation is insoluble. But the fact that we are complaining should persuade us to reexamine those assumptions. Particularly because with our Great Physician, nothing is impossible (Matthew 19:26).

5. The Great Physician may have different plans.

Consider Paul's thorn in the flesh. In 2 Corinthians 12:7, he says, "I was given a thorn in my flesh, a messenger of Satan, to torment me." Paul doesn't tell us what that problem was. Perhaps he left out the details because the Holy Spirit wanted to create a fill-in-the-blank opportunity for the rest of us. In place of "thorn in my flesh," we can write in "cancer" or whatever burden cripples us.

Paul interpreted his thorn as a hindrance to his ability to serve the Savior. He wanted it purged from his life. He was frustrated because it diminished his capacity for ministry. Not once or twice but three times Paul pleaded with Jesus to take it away.

But the LORD had no plans to remove the thorn from Paul's flesh. The thorn would stay to remind the apostle of the most valuable portion of his inventory. God's grace would more than overcome the damage this thorn could inflict.

Jesus gave Paul an unexpected answer to his prayer: "My grace is sufficient for you, for my power is made perfect in weakness" (2 Corinthians 12:9). No, Paul, Jesus told him, I won't take your problem away. That problem will keep you focused on the power of my undeserved love for you. That problem will demonstrate how powerful and loving I am. That problem will turn out to be no problem, because I will accomplish astounding things through you in spite of it.

When Paul took a personal inventory, he discovered he had something of much greater value than he had realized. His inventory transformed his ministry. He explains, "I will boast all the more gladly about my weaknesses, so that Christ's power may rest on me. That is why, for Christ's sake, I delight in weaknesses, in insults, in hardships, in persecutions, in difficulties. For when I am weak, then I am strong" (2 Corinthians 12:9,10).

God had a similar message to share with Jeremiah's contemporaries who were forced into exile. They begged God to allow them to return home. The Lord had better plans. They would settle across the Babylonian Empire. They would not be able to return to Jerusalem for 70 years. In that time, the Spirit would use them as a light to a sin-darkened nation. God explained, "I know the plans I have for you, . . . plans to prosper you and not to harm you, plans to give you hope and a future" (Jeremiah 29:11).

God's plans for the exiles didn't match the plan the exiles had. God's plans became their thorn in the flesh. Like Paul, they were forced to reevaluate their situation. They had to take an inventory.

The Lord used Jeremiah's complaints to prompt the prophet's personal inventory. "Oh, that my head were a spring of water and my eyes a fountain of tears!" Jeremiah whined. "I would weep day and night for the slain of my people" (Jeremiah 9:1). Jeremiah's mourning over his people brought him to submit his resignation: "Oh, that I had in the desert a lodging place for travelers, so that I might leave my people and go away from them; for they are all adulterers, a crowd of unfaithful people" (Jeremiah 9:2).

God responded, Jeremiah, you've forgotten the blessings you have in me. I've got this handled. "You live in the midst of deception; in their deceit they refuse to acknowledge me. Should I not punish them for this? . . . Should I not avenge myself on such a nation as this?" (Jeremiah 9:6,9). I'm not removing your thorn in the flesh, the Lord was telling Jeremiah. I am using it to keep you focused on your true source of comfort. I'm using it to rivet your attention on me.

So yes, complain that you have cancer. Grumble about the uncertainty, the discomfort, the fear. But recognize that grumbling is not an end. It is only the first step toward whatever lesson your Father is teaching. Take inventory.

Complaining is the starting point in a journey that leads to appropriate action. It must become a land we travel through. It is never a destination. Grousing about a situation is never a remedy for that situation. It is an indication that we are in a predicament beyond our ability to manage and we are searching for some help. It reminds us that only a closer connection with the God of unlimited power and grace will bring an antidote.

> Recognize that grumbling is not an end. It is only the first step toward whatever lesson your Father is teaching.

Prayer

Father of constant comfort, keep me focused on your Jesus-won commitment to me. Empower me to embrace my complaints as a tool you will use to shower me with greater blessings. Silence my sighs and cries. Open my ears to your assurance that your mercies are new every morning and your faithfulness cannot be measured (Lamentations 3:23). Amen.

Chapter 4

WHERE AM I FOCUSING MY ATTENTION?

The problem with June bugs

Early summer driving in Wisconsin's countryside provides beautiful green vistas set against blue skies dabbed with puffs of cloud. We rejoice in the dramatic change from winter's interminably dreary drabness.

But May and June are also the months when summer's insects dominate. This includes June bugs, the B-52 bombers of the insect world. These hulking beetles seem drawn to highways, especially at night. There, kamikaze-like, they seem to hurl themselves against windshields, spattering like overripe mini watermelons.

> Complaints are like June bug splotches on a windshield. They insist we focus on the ugliness of life rather than the beauty.

The next day the windshield is a mess. I'm always surprised when I find my attention attracted more to the beetle goo on my windshield than to the fields and forests beyond. What is it about a hit-and-splat collision with a June bug that demands more eyeball time than the Wisconsin summer landscape?

Let me make a comparison: Complaints are like June bug splotches on a windshield. They insist we focus on the ugliness of life rather than the beauty. On what exasperates rather than what fascinates. On what outrages rather than what is outstanding. Grousing about what's wrong tends to keep us focused on the problem; it can hinder us from moving toward a solution.

What happens is what I call catastrophic thinking. That occurs when we experience uncontrollable anxiety over an imagined life-threatening crisis. Of course, it is reasonable to feel anxious in the face of an actual threat. But the catastrophe happens when we think the worst will happen even when it is only a remote possibility.

A sure sign that catastrophic thinking has captured you in its web is using words like *always, never, nothing, nobody, everybody*. For example, "*Nobody* cares. *Nothing* ever goes right for me. My life is worse than *everyone else's* life."

For a number of weeks when my children were in high school, each day they would come home, slam their books down on the kitchen table, and moan, "This was the worst day ever!" I would often respond, "I thought yesterday was the worst day ever."

"No! Today is the worst day ever!" they'd say in unison. Their eye rolls and slow head shakes made it clear that our conversation had run its course. Explaining the daily catastrophe of teenage life to a father was a fruitless endeavor.

Catastrophic thinking

Catastrophic thinking is at the heart of Jeremiah's lament in Lamentations 1:12: "Is any suffering like my suffering that was inflicted on me, that the LORD brought on me in the day of his fierce anger?"

Notice the words *all* and *everyone* in this rant: "I am ridiculed *all* day long; *everyone* mocks me. Whenever I speak, I cry out proclaiming violence and destruction. So the word of the LORD has brought me insult and reproach *all* day long. *All* my friends are waiting for me to slip" (Jeremiah 20:7,8,10, emphasis added).

Because of Jeremiah's catastrophic thinking, he felt justified for denouncing the God who orchestrated his birth. "Cursed be the man who brought my father the news, who made him very glad, saying, 'A child is born to you—a son!' May that man be like the towns the LORD overthrew without pity. May he hear wailing in the morning, a battle cry at noon. For he did not kill me in the womb, with my mother as my grave, her womb enlarged forever. Why did I ever come out of the womb to see trouble and sorrow and to end my days in shame?" (Jeremiah 20:15-18).

There is something remarkable here, however. In this section of Jeremiah chapter 20, the prophet wrestles to pull his eyes from the June bug blotch. He forces himself to proclaim, "The LORD is with me like a mighty warrior; so my persecutors will stumble and not prevail. Sing to the LORD! Give praise to the LORD! He rescues the life of the needy from the hands of the wicked" (Jeremiah 20:11,13). Yet Jeremiah struggles to unshackle himself from his catastrophic thinking, or what I'd also call "stinkin' thinkin.'" He continues, "Cursed be the day I was born! May the day my mother bore me not be blessed!" (Jeremiah 20:14).

Catastrophic thinking flows from our flawed and sinful nature. We struggle as the apostle Paul struggled: "I do not do the good I want to do, but the evil I do not want to do—this I keep on doing" (Romans 7:19). We should trust in the love of our God, but we do not and keep on with our doubts, fears, and stinkin' thinkin.'

How did that happen? We think about an event or the news we either hear or anticipate, and we assign some value to it. We may choose to define an event as good or bad, beneficial or detrimental, desired or deplored. Based on the value we assign to an event, our emotions tell us how to feel. And based on how we feel about a situation, we react. If we interpret an event as threatening, our emotions will launch a fight-or-flight reaction. If we choose to view an event as welcomed or easily manageable, our emotions will suggest a more positive response.

The problem with catastrophic thinking is that it bullies us into skipping the logical interpretation of an event and abandoning God's promises. We move directly from event to feeling. And since we're anticipating a catastrophe, that feeling is always negative, defensive, and excessive. That's why our reaction can be extreme, even outrageous, and we slide away from the comfort and strength of God's promises.

Overcoming catastrophic thinking

The key to overcoming catastrophic thinking is realizing that it is not logical and it abandons the positive alternative of the LORD. What we need to do is short-circuit those thoughts. Some people force themselves to take a deep breath. Or two or three. Counting to 10 may clear away the craziness. Much better than either of those approaches is praying.

> Pray until you can consider your situation based on your status as a heaven-bound saint.

Pray until your head clears to the point that you can respond logically and confidently to your predicament. Pray until you can consider your situation based on your status as a heaven-bound saint. Listen to Jeremiah's prayer: "You deceived me, LORD, and I was deceived. . . . I am ridiculed all day long; everyone mocks me" (Jeremiah 20:7). Yes, it's a complaint. But it is a prayer. He speaks to the LORD. It's a step on the way to clearing his mind.

Notice what Jeremiah does next. He attempts to recapture his believer's mind by clinging to scriptural truths the Spirit inspired through earlier writers. "The LORD is with me like a mighty warrior," he says. Therefore his "persecutors will stumble and not prevail" (Jeremiah 20:11). His thought is not an isolated hope in the middle of his troubles. Note how similar Jeremiah's words are to those of the prophet Zephaniah, a contemporary of Jeremiah: "The LORD your God is with you, the Mighty Warrior who saves" (Zephaniah 3:17). And the words of Isaiah: "The LORD will march out like a champion, like a warrior he will stir up his zeal; with a shout he will raise the battle cry and will triumph over his enemies" (Isaiah 42:13).

Open your Bible when stinkin' thinkin' assaults you. The Spirit transforms your thinking through contact with his Word. Since "faith comes from hearing the message, and the message is heard through the word about Christ" (Romans 10:17), flee to the Scriptures when catastrophic thinking seeks to rule your mind. Allow your Father to assure you that you are fully forgiven. Keep reading until his promise that you are fully accepted and loved by him takes over.

> Open your Bible when stinkin' thinkin' assaults you.

Paul urges, "Do not conform to the pattern of this world," which focuses on the June bug splat rather than the beauty of God's grace. Rather, "be transformed by the renewing of your mind," by the new thinking that the Scriptures work in you. "Then you will be able to test and approve what God's will is—his good, pleasing and perfect will" (Romans 12:2).

Renewed by the truth of the Almighty's allegiance, the prophet then moves to another weapon in the believer's arsenal: praise. "Sing to the LORD! Give praise to the LORD!" he urges his soul (Jeremiah 20:13). Jeremiah is practicing what Paul urged the early churches to do: "Give thanks in all circumstances" (1 Thessalonians 5:18) and "rejoice in the Lord always" (Philippians 4:4).

There is excellent logic behind praising God, even when nothing seems praiseworthy. The prophet confesses, "He rescues the life of the needy from the hands of the wicked" (Jeremiah 20:13). God's rescue of his people is as dependable as the next tick of time. For that we can praise him, even when the certainty of the next second, day, or even year seems doubtful.

The reason Jeremiah could be sure of God's rescue was the LORD's commitment to forgive all his sins. A century before Jeremiah, the Spirit used Isaiah to explain how we need never fear. He wrote, "This is what the LORD says—he who created you, Jacob, he who formed you, Israel: 'Do not fear, for I have redeemed you; I have summoned you by name; you are mine. When you pass through the waters, I will be with you; and when you pass through the rivers, they will not sweep over you. When you walk through the fire, you will not be burned; the flames will not set you ablaze. For I am the LORD your God, the Holy One of Israel, your Savior'" (Isaiah 43:1-3).

> The reason Jeremiah could be sure of God's rescue was the LORD's commitment to forgive all his sins.

The LORD has redeemed us, adopted us, and treasures us. God makes this same promise to you. Jesus has underwritten that promise.

Jeremiah's attempt to manage his catastrophic view of his situation was exemplary. Unfortunately, he lapsed and did not continue. "Cursed be the day I was born!" he laments (Jeremiah 20:14). Jeremiah's gaze returned to the bug splat on his windshield rather than the beauty of God's grace surrounding him.

I cannot estimate the times I have tried to drown my complaints in God's promises only to have them resurface. Along with Jeremiah, I've discovered how slippery complaints are. Do you also sense it? How often have your complaints wriggled out of control only to bob back up to plague you?

How do we recover when our complaints refuse to drown? We keep returning to the place where Jeremiah found the strength to hold down his grumbling: "The LORD is with me like a mighty warrior; so my persecutors will stumble and not prevail" (Jeremiah 20:11). That is truth; it never changes. No matter how many times our emotions insist we curse our birth, the LORD's relationship with us has not changed. "He rescues the life of the needy from the hands of the wicked" (Jeremiah 20:13).

Overcoming guilt

Of course, in the face of failure, choosing to "sing to the LORD" and "give praise to the LORD" is difficult (Jeremiah 20:13). It is even more daunting when we are grieving over sin in our lives. Jeremiah encountered that: "See, LORD, how distressed I am! I am in torment within, and in my heart I am disturbed, for I have been most rebellious. Outside, the sword bereaves; inside, there is only death" (Lamentations 1:20).

Cancer encourages feelings of guilt. The "if onlys" or "I should haves" haunt. We anguish over the fears our loved ones tremble under because of our trouble. We may feel remorse because we realize we caused our cancer. We smoked. We didn't go to the doctor soon enough. We explained away the symptoms. We didn't do what we were told to do. The list is long.

A cancer survivor told me, "When I think about having cancer, I see the things for which I beat on myself. First of all, I was really down on myself that I didn't find this sooner. What if this had really taken off when it didn't have to. And then really feeling guilty for my husband. What if I put him through all of this and it wouldn't have been necessary. It would have caused him more pain and me just looking bad."

Guilt makes cancer into Sleepy Hollow's headless horseman. But there is no specter galloping toward us. Take a breath. Open the Bible and listen to Jeremiah. Say the words with him, "The LORD is with me like a mighty warrior" (Jeremiah 20:11).

The LORD's commitment

When the volume on our complaints is dialed to ear-shattering, when culpability for the mess we've caused screams for our punishment, listen to hear God's name. "Yahweh," he speaks. "Know that Yahweh is here with arms open wide. No matter what else shouts for your attention, know my love for you is great, higher than the heavens." No hint of anger remains in my heart, he tells us. No matter how blatant your rebellion. No matter how stunning your failure. No matter how dark the days seem.

The truth of God's grace in Jesus calls for our attention. Paul reminded the Romans, "Since we have been justified through faith, we have peace with God through our Lord Jesus Christ, through whom we have gained access by faith into this grace in which we now stand" (Romans 5:1,2). Did you notice the verbs? They describe actions that have already happened. Those actions cannot be undone. We have been justified. We have peace with God. We have gained access to grace.

> The truth of God's grace in Jesus calls for our attention.

Think through the picture in Paul's description of our status before God. He writes about the "grace in which we now stand." Because of Jesus, we no longer must grovel before God. We stand because his grace has given us that status. We are enveloped in his grace. Wherever we are, whatever we are doing, and no matter the circumstances, through Jesus we are surrounded by, cleansed by, and empowered by God's unlimited love for us.

"Since we have been justified through faith, . . . we boast in the hope of the glory of God," Paul exults (Romans 5:1,2). Our standing in God's grace here will bring us to stand in the glory of God's heaven one day. Fully accepted. Eternally safe. Far beyond the reach of any suffering.

Based on our standing with God now and the glories of heaven that await, our troubles here are transformed. "Not only so," Paul continues, "but we also glory in our sufferings, because we know that suffering produces perseverance; perseverance, character; and character, hope" (Romans 5:3,4).

Even in the most challenging of times, even in Jeremiah-like suffering, even in the face of terminal cancer, God's grace in Jesus produces perseverance, character, and hope. His grace swaddles us, soothing away the temptation to complain and helping us grow in our trust in him.

Overpower the voice of catastrophic thinking

To shift focus away from whatever is troubling us to God's grace requires that we overpower the voice of fear and catastrophic thinking. That battle is fierce. Our fear gives our emotions a voice that never tires. Its harangue is incessant. Jeremiah demonstrated how savage the conflict can become.

It's as if we're on a trip from Chicago to Germany flying in the economy class and enduring an infant's shrieks for most of our 4,000-mile journey. His wailing distracts us from work, ruins our conversations, sours our meals, and makes sleep impossible. Headphones at full volume offer the only reprieve.

The emotions our fears create are like that infant. Theirs is a voice that can never be silenced, but it can be outshouted. So cheer for the LORD. Huzzah until hoarse. Shout his promises of hope and peace. Drown out the voice that speaks of impending catastrophe. Make sure his voice is in your headphones.

This requires allowing our Father to speak to us—at full volume, without pause. He speaks to us in his Word. God's Word provides the armor we require to stand against any assault. "Put on the full armor of God," Paul urges, "so that when the day of evil comes, you may be able to stand your ground, and after you have done everything, to stand." Dressed in that armor, not even "the flaming arrows of the evil one" will find their mark (Ephesians 6:13,16).

We can also drown out that voice when we surround ourselves with Christian mentors who will support us, guide us, and pray with us. Invite them into your life. Find believers who are "filled with the Spirit" and can share with you what the Spirit has given them through the "psalms, hymns, and songs from the Spirit." Join them as they "sing and make music from [the] heart to the Lord, always giving thanks to God the Father for everything, in the name of our Lord Jesus Christ" (Ephesians 5:18-20).

When my complaints shout the loudest, I've found it hardest to seek the encouragement of other Christians. I tell myself that no one will understand. Others will minimize my pain. They will reject me. I'm embarrassed to admit to anyone I'm struggling with this. But those thoughts are lies. They allow my complaints to resurface. They keep me chained to my fears and false assumptions about my circumstances.

> Find other Christians who will help you hold those complaints down and lift Jesus up.

Here's the lesson: Don't believe them. Find other Christians who will help you hold those complaints down and lift Jesus up.

Another help is prayer. Speak with your Father about your struggles, your dreams, your frustrations, your goals. Tell him about life's unfairness, about why you can't seem to overcome your catastrophic thinking, about your impression that he is mistreating you. Complain to him. He won't mind. He will listen. And though he may not agree, he will understand.

Pray like anguished David: "In you, LORD my God, I put my trust. Guide me in your truth and teach me, for you are God my Savior. My eyes are ever on the LORD, for only he will release my feet from the snare. Turn to me and be gracious to me, for I am lonely and afflicted. Relieve the troubles of my heart and free me from my anguish" (Psalm 25:1,5,15-17).

A spiritual hero

One of the strengths of Jeremiah that I appreciate is his spiritual tenacity. While deep in battle with the lying voice of his fears and anguish, he refused to release his faith-grip on the LORD's promises. The assault of his spiritual weaknesses knocked him onto his heels and brought him to complain. But the gospel never allowed him to desert his faith and hope in the LORD.

How often I need that example. The threats of cancer—or any other hardship—may overwhelm my heart with thoughts of catastrophe. But the war is not lost, I've learned. I've only lost a skirmish. In the power of my Father's grace, I can armor up and fight again. Jesus has already won the war for me.

In the time surrounding my first bout with cancer, my daily prayers included a petition I had never before felt the need to speak: "LORD, help me view my life based on the truths I know by faith rather than the lies I hear from my fears and anguish." What lies assaulted me! "Your God doesn't care about you. Pastor Aderman, everything you have taught others is a lie. You are worse than wrong; you are worthless."

How strange, I thought, that I could understand how my Savior is my ever-present help in trouble and yet I could still feel lost in the wilderness. How strange that these lies could exist in the same space as the assurances of God's grace.

My Father allowed that struggle to go on for many months. He taught me, when these doubting shouts filled my days, to strain to listen to what often seemed the still, small voice of the gospel. "Did Jesus die on the cross?" I'd ask myself. "Did he rise from the dead?" "Yes. Yes. No matter how I feel about God failing me, Jesus died for me; he rose again. That is a fact of history. Therefore, my God loves me. My God will keep his promises to me." I did not always feel God's love, but I clung to the words because they are true.

I think of Jeremiah complaining at what the LORD had done to him and his people. I am like him, but there is no need to stay there, wallowing in complaint. "I know that my redeemer lives," the grieving Job declares. Like Jeremiah, he refused to succumb to his heart-lies. "In the end [my redeemer] will stand on the earth," he continues. "And after my skin has been destroyed, yet in my flesh I will see God" (Job 19:25,26). "Here *I* stand."

> Refuse to spend energy looking at the bug splatter on your windshield.

Refuse to spend energy looking at the bug splatter on your windshield. God's grace—certified at the cross and tomb—provides an awesome panorama to marvel at, to rejoice over. Like Jeremiah, battle to keep your focus there. "The LORD is with me like a mighty warrior; so my persecutors will stumble and not prevail. Sing to the LORD! Give praise to the LORD! He rescues the life of the needy from the hands of the wicked" (Jeremiah 20:11,13).

Prayer

Father of unending grace, I confess that I lose my focus on your love. I am lured away from the voice of your Word by the voice of my fears and anguish. Forgive me. Take my focus away from life's upsets and center it on your beauty, your promises, and your Son. Use the sound of your Scriptures to drown out the lies that arise within me. Never allow me to forget that you are with me like a mighty warrior. You rescue my life from the hands of the wicked. You will always be that God for me because the Redeemer you sent for me lives—now and forever. Amen.

Additional prayers: The Psalms offer many prayers by anguished believers. Use them to give a voice to your complaints and to bring new focus to your Father's love for you. For example, read Psalms 22,31,74,85,142.

Chapter 5
WHO DIRECTS WHAT I THINK?

Phil McDowell died on December 13, 2017. His death at age 47 touched hundreds of lives. A ten-year-old girl in his congregation wrote about her grief:

> Mr. McDowell.
> What a shame.
> I hate to hear his name.
> I shout to God, "Why him? Why him?"
> Because I miss him so.

Not just ten-year-olds become exasperated with God. Chances are you have argued with him over your cancer: "Father, this isn't right! I had plans! I had plans to serve you, plans to travel, plans to enjoy life. This isn't right. My family depends on me. My career is just taking off. Now you've ruined all of that."

The people of Jeremiah's Judah were infuriated with the LORD. They were frustrated because the LORD did not fulfill their expectations. They viewed the LORD as their marionette. In their minds, they were not the children of God; they were his puppet master. They manipulated the strings, and God was required to dance in tune with their song. These people believed they knew what was best. Since God was not providing it, they believed God had failed them.

The heart's deceit

No wonder the LORD warns, "Cursed is the one who trusts in man, who draws strength from mere flesh and whose heart turns away from the LORD" (Jeremiah 17:5). The reason we can't trust our own judgment? "The heart is deceitful above all things and beyond cure. Who can understand it?" (Jeremiah 17:9). Oscar Wilde was a man of many gifts. Theology was not one of them. He quipped, "I think God, in creating man, somewhat overestimated his ability." Wilde should have spent time reading the Bible.

God is aware of our capacity for evil. Jeremiah offers 52 chapters of evidence. We provide our own evidence whenever we believe God would do well to take directions from us. The people of Jerusalem complained because they thought they knew better than the Almighty. They allowed the wrong lord to direct their thinking. Such faulty thinking also accounts for some of Jeremiah's complaints. And ours.

There's an escape from thinking we are God's puppet master. Jeremiah chapter 18 provides the way out.

God as the potter

The LORD directed Jeremiah, "Go down to the potter's house, and there I will give you my message" (Jeremiah 18:2). At the potter's house, the prophet watched as the potter, hands gloved in gray mud, massaged the clay on his wheel. But the pot was marred as he worked on it. "The potter formed it into another pot, shaping it as seemed best to him" (Jeremiah 18:4). The LORD explained his object lesson: "Can I not do with you, Israel, as this potter does? . . . Like clay in the hand of the potter, so are you in my hand, Israel" (Jeremiah 18:6).

This is the bottom line of this exercise in pottery-making: The LORD is our Creator. He spoke, and the universe came into existence thousands of years ago. Since then, every second he has nurtured and cultivated the cosmos in all its unimaginable vastness. On this small planet, he fashioned you and me out of just the right genetic materials in our mothers' wombs. He brought us into his world in just the right place, at just the right time, and for just the right reason.

As our Creator, the LORD has the right to choose how to position us for our role in life and how to steer us through life. He works the clay; he shapes the pot for whatever purpose he determines. Isaiah reminds us of the lesson that we should remember our place: "You turn things upside down, as if the potter were thought to be like the clay! Shall what is formed say to the one who formed it, 'You did not make me'? Can the pot say to the potter, 'You know nothing'?" (Isaiah 29:16).

> As our Creator, the LORD has the right to choose how to position us for our role in life and how to steer us through life. He works the clay.

In God's plan for our lives, we pots don't have a vote. We don't even have a voice.

LORD (Yahweh)

Remember that we are using the capitalized name of God, LORD, to identify the name of God, Yahweh, as used in the Hebrew Bible. God uses that name to emphasize his graciousness. He used it twice when he spoke to Moses: "The LORD, the LORD, the compassionate and gracious God, slow to anger, abounding in love and faithfulness" (Exodus 34:6).

It's the name Jeremiah uses in the opening verse of chapter 18. Because of the LORD's abounding love and faithfulness, we find comfort in his pottery-making. Even when we don't understand why he has shaped us into the pots that we are, we can confess with Isaiah, "Yet you, LORD, are our Father. We are the clay, you are the potter; we are all the work of your hand" (Isaiah 64:8).

We are the work of God's hands. But he has done more than shape us and place us where he wants us. He sent his Son to be nailed to a cross in order to transform us from sinners into saints—to transform us from the captives of Satan into his infinitely loved sons and daughters. Beyond that eternal transformation, the Potter has transformed us into creatures who bring him glory while we live here. The LORD has chosen to shape us physically, emotionally, and intellectually so we are the exact instrument needed to accomplish what he wants done when he wants it done.

But don't miss this: The decisions the Potter has made in shaping us all flow from his heart, from a "love that surpasses knowledge" (Ephesians 3:19). What he has done for us in Jesus certifies the limitlessness of his love.

Our Potter can never be capricious in the way he directs our lives. His decisions are always determined by his undeserved love for us. The grace that saved us is the grace that guides us. That's why Paul can ask, "He who did not spare his own Son, but gave him up for us all—how will he not also, along with him, graciously give us all things?" (Romans 8:32).

Struggling against the Potter

Yet we struggle with allowing our gift-giving Father the right to direct our lives. Like the Israelites—like Jeremiah—we argue with him about the decisions he makes for our lives. We find fault with his choice to bring cancer into our lives. We struggle to submit to our Father's will. We choose instead to demand our own preferences. We want God to do what we want.

> We struggle with allowing our gift-giving Father the right to direct our lives.

Anne Lamott quipped, "The difference between you and God is that God doesn't think he's you." When we think we are God, when we think we know better than God, we complain. We complain about our cancer and any other challenge.

At times Jeremiah forgot that difference between himself and God. He struggled to be at peace with the shape into which the Potter molded him. In the opening verses of chapter 15, the LORD commanded his prophet to predict the merciless destruction of his people. God said to tell them, "I will send four kinds of destroyers against them, . . . the sword to kill and the dogs to drag away and the birds and the wild animals to devour and destroy" (Jeremiah 15:3). Jeremiah bewails his role as a doomsday prophet: "Alas, my mother, that you gave me birth, a man with whom the whole land strives and contends! I have neither lent nor borrowed, yet everyone curses me" (Jeremiah 15:10).

But Jeremiah battles to regain his faith-footing. "LORD, you understand," he says, "remember me and care for me. Avenge me on my persecutors. You are long-suffering—do not take me away; think of how I suffer reproach for your sake" (Jeremiah 15:15). Unfortunately, Jeremiah's best intentions fade, because in the next breath he forgets that the gracious LORD is the Potter and he is the clay: "Why is my pain unending and my wound grievous and incurable? You are to me like a deceptive brook, like a spring that fails" (Jeremiah 15:18).

Lamentations contains similar examples of finding fault with the Potter (see Lamentations 2:4,5; 3:1-5). The anguish came when Jeremiah thought he knew better than God about how his life should unfold. For believers of all times, it is a struggle to trust our Father's plans for us, especially when his plans run counter to our own.

"It's not fair," the mother of a dying middle-aged man told me. He laid next to us on his deathbed. Within two days his cancer would take his life. "He's so young," his mother sobbed. We talked about the glories of heaven that awaited him. But in that moment, she found little in that thought to ease her pain. Talk of God's goodness seemed to be a deceptive brook.

As you have wrestled with cancer, you probably haven't labeled God a liar and a failure like Jeremiah did. Nonetheless, gainsaying the Potter's judgment requires no effort when you think that:

- God has taken away what you value most.
- God has shown none of the love and power for which he wants you to know him.
- God has failed to answer your prayers.
- God has consigned you to a hellhole with no way out short of death.

Walk by faith

When Paul writes that we live by faith rather than by sight (2 Corinthians 5:7), he's describing an important life principle. Faith in Jesus insists that we deny what *we* think is best and embrace what our Savior has determined is best.

I admire my wife for the astounding number of gifts the Spirit has given her. For example, she is a remarkably loving person. The proof is she has committed herself to me for a half century. Yet she lacks a sense of direction. A compass in her car and a voice on her GPS have helped a lot. I tease her when she has to find her own way by saying that she would be better off turning the opposite direction from the way she thinks she should go. By birth, not one of us has a dependable spiritual sense of direction, so we must walk in the direction that faith in God's grace gives us.

Martin Luther said this about overcoming the temptation to trust his own spiritual sense of direction: "I must comfort myself in such terror and fear, pull myself together by faith, and say to the devil and to my heart: 'You frighten me with sin and hell, but Christ tells me of heaven, righteousness, life, and eternal bliss. He must have greater weight with me than all my feelings and ideas.' And thus we must ever struggle and resist, firmly holding and clinging to this article. This will be necessary both in life and in death." (*Luther's Works*, Vol. 28, p. 106).

That principle of giving God's Word "greater weight . . . than all my feelings and ideas" is alive in Jeremiah chapter 32. The Babylonian army surrounded Jerusalem. Nothing came into the city; nothing left. People starved. Commandoes would breach the walls. Defeat was imminent. Everyone saw that.

In the face of impending annihilation, the LORD told Jeremiah to purchase a plot of ground. But such a purchase made no sense. Why would someone buy land that the Babylonians would soon control? It would be history's worst investment. Except Jeremiah wrote, "I knew that this was the word of the LORD; so I bought the field" (Jeremiah 32:8,9). Then the word of the LORD came to him again: "I am the LORD, the God of all mankind. Is anything too hard for me? I will bring [my people] back to this place and let them live in safety. Fields will be bought . . . deeds will be signed, sealed and witnessed" (Jeremiah 32:27,37,44). Jeremiah's purchase of property was to be a testimony that God would keep his promise to restore Jerusalem's fortunes.

Jeremiah obeyed, even though it seemed foolish. Driven by faith rather than by sight, he confessed his Creator could—and would—do what he had promised. "Ah, Sovereign LORD," Jeremiah writes, "you have made the heavens and the earth by your great power and outstretched arm. Nothing is too hard for you" (Jeremiah 32:17).

"Nothing is too hard for you." When God is not directing you down the road you would have chosen, hold to those words. Nothing is too hard for our God. No pain is so excruciating that our God can't eliminate it in a moment. No disease is so virulent that the LORD can't vanquish it. Turn where he tells you. Nothing is too hard for him.

Of course, that does not mean our Father will use his omnipotence to save us from surgery or chemotherapy or radiation treatments. It does not mean he will cure our cancer so we can go on with our plans.

Jeremiah bought property because of God's promise that life would one day return to normal in Judah. It soon seemed, however, that God's promise had failed. The Babylonians did

59

destroy Jerusalem and slaughter much of its population. They forced many into exile. But according to God's promise, the exiles returned 70 years later—as God predicted—to rebuild the temple, the city, and their country, as well as their vineyards, fields, and houses.

> He has a place in his house waiting for you.

God calls on us to purchase property when we are faced with cancer's fierce enemies, who are about to breach our walls. "Trust my promises," he urges. "Trust me, not your own limited intellect. Nothing is too hard for me." He has a place in his house waiting for you (John 14:2,3).

The foundation for our trust

We know we can trust him because the King of kings has conquered all enemies for us. He shed his blood to rescue us from them. He rose from death to signal his eternal victory and our eternal life. He now rules in heaven because he is the "great and mighty God, whose name is the LORD Almighty." Jeremiah must be correct when he says, "Great are your purposes and mighty are your deeds" (Jeremiah 32:18,19).

Whatever the Potter's plans are for you, nothing is too hard for him. He will do for you what his loving potter's heart chooses to do. What the Potter has done for us through his Son shows that is the case. "This is how God showed his love among us: He sent his one and only Son into the world that we might live through him. This is love: not that we loved God, but that he loved us and sent his Son as an atoning sacrifice for our sins" (1 John 4:9,10).

A Christian sister found her footing on that promise when she learned she had cancer. She told me, "My greatest fear was telling my kids that I have breast cancer. I was concerned that they might feel frightened because Mom has this. I reassured them that God loves me and that he knows what's best for me."

God also assured Jeremiah that he knew what was best. In the same chapter as Jeremiah's pottery lesson, we hear the LORD God encourage his prophet, "I am with you to rescue and save you.... I will save you from the hands of the wicked and deliver you from the grasp of the cruel" (Jeremiah 15:20,21). In other words, God says, "No matter how unredeemable this situation seems, I have it under control. I will keep my promises. Listen to me, not to yourself."

Isaiah has the same lesson for us. He wrote, "This is what the LORD says—he who created you, Jacob, he who formed you, Israel: 'Do not fear, for I have redeemed you; I have summoned you by name; you are mine. When you pass through the waters, I will be with you; and when you pass through the rivers, they will not sweep over you. When you walk through the fire, you will not be burned; the flames will not set you ablaze. For I am the LORD your God, the Holy One of Israel, your Savior'" (Isaiah 43:1-3).

> Whatever the Potter's plans are for you, nothing is too hard for him. He will do for you what his loving potter's heart chooses to do.

So certain is the Potter's loving care for us that the Scriptures urge:

- "Give thanks in all circumstances; for this is God's will for you in Christ Jesus" (1 Thessalonians 5:18).
- "Consider it pure joy, my brothers and sisters, whenever you face trials of many kinds" (James 1:2).
- "Do not make light of the Lord's discipline, and do not lose heart when he rebukes you, because the Lord disciplines the one he loves, and he chastens everyone he accepts as his son" (Hebrews 12:5,6).

Grace taught Corrie ten Boom to trust the Potter. She suffered the worst that the Nazi concentration camps inflicted. Her book about that experience, *The Hiding Place*, was named not only for the room where her family hid Jews from the Germans but also for her God. The King James Version of Psalm 119:114 reads, "Thou art my hiding place and my shield: I hope in thy word." Ten Boom writes of that hiding place, "Never be afraid to trust an unknown future to a known God."

Overcoming faulty thinking

In Jeremiah, we've seen how faulty thinking prompts complaints. Let's also investigate how God provides us the victory over that thinking.

When the prophet groused about how God chose to use him, the LORD patiently explained, "If you repent, I will restore you that you may serve me; if you utter worthy, not worthless, words, you will be my spokesman. Let this people turn to you, but you must not turn to them. I will make you a wall to this people, a fortified wall of bronze; they will fight against you but will not overcome you, for I am with you to rescue and save you. . . . I will save you from the hands of the wicked and deliver you from the grasp of the cruel" (Jeremiah 15:19-21).

Here God sets out three principles for the prophet and us that will empower us to overcome our dependence on our faulty reasoning instead of God's wisdom. Those principles are repentance, recommitment, and response.

Repentance

God called his grumbling spokesman to repent: "If you repent, I will restore you that you may serve me" (Jeremiah 15:19). The first step in honoring God's leadership in our lives and turning away from our dependence on our own thinking is acknowledging our sin.

> God called his grumbling spokesman to repent.

God has provided forgiveness in Jesus for all humanity. It stands like a refreshing fountain of cool water for all to drink. The people in Judah and Jerusalem had a rich history of the refreshing water of life. God had brought them from Egypt, given them a land of their own, and promised that the Savior would come into the world through them. But now they had forgotten all that. They had rebelled and chosen other gods. Their thinking was no longer on the promises of God. Jeremiah called them to repent. When they did, God promised he would refresh their spirits again.

Unfortunately, the people refused to admit rebellion against God's will. Therefore, weeping over what seemed to be nonexistent sin made no sense. The result: Their spiritual deadness demanded God's severe punishment.

Jeremiah's experience with the same sin produced a different outcome. "If you repent," God promised him, "I will restore you that you may serve me" (Jeremiah 15:19). The Hebrew word for "repent" (*shub*) means "to turn back, to return." It's the word used in Hosea 6:1: "Come, let us return to the LORD. He has torn us to pieces but he will heal us; he has injured us but he will bind up our wounds." Jeremiah wrote about his turning back, "After I strayed, I repented; after I came to understand, I beat my breast. I was ashamed and humiliated because I bore the disgrace of my youth" (Jeremiah 31:19).

But what has happened to us? Do we need to hear the words inviting us to return to the LORD's refreshing promises? In the face of our troubles and trials, we wonder if the blessings and comforts he offers are true and real or only an illusion. Our sinful human hearts deceive us, and we blame him, complain, desert his blessings, and seek our own solutions. We want another god who will give us what we want instead of what we need. We harbor faulty thinking and grumble.

Our journey from the sin of faulting our Father to our return to trusting in him begins with thinking clearly about who we are and who God is. It begins with becoming like the prodigal son of Jesus' parable who came to his senses and returned to his father.

It begins with acknowledging that we valued our meandering to a distant country more than we loved our Father's home.

God called Jerusalem and Jeremiah to repent. On some level, God is using your cancer to lead you to recognize your faulty thinking about him. He is calling you to turn back to him. If you even have doubts about him now, he challenges you to hold on more firmly as you face the days ahead. There's always that little voice inside that wants us to question our heavenly Father. Admitting these sins and even the inclination to grouse about God requires launching an honest investigation into the reason for your skewed concept of God. Should you also confess you are a clay pot that has found fault with the Potter? Do you need to admit you are a lost sheep that has chosen your own way rather than your Shepherd's way?

Then tell your Father about that. Now is a good time. Tell him not only with sorrow but also with confidence. He is more than willing to forgive. His love for you never diminishes. It is always that cool, refreshing stream of love and forgiveness. Yes, sometimes we have refused to drink from it, but it is always there.

Our God never hesitates to forgive our sins. He promised Jerusalem and Judah, "I will cleanse them from all the sin they have committed against me and will forgive all their sins of rebellion against me" (Jeremiah 33:8).

How is that possible? He has signed that pledge in his Son's blood. "I will make an everlasting covenant with them," he told Jeremiah. "I will never stop doing good to them, and I will inspire them to fear me, so that they will never turn away from me. I will rejoice in doing them good and will assuredly plant them in this land with all my heart and soul" (Jeremiah 32:40,41).

Recommitment

The first principle is to repent, to turn back to the LORD and his promises. "If you repent," God told Jeremiah, "I will restore you that you may serve me." The LORD goes on, "If you utter worthy, not worthless, words, you will be my spokesman. Let this people turn to you, but you must not turn to them" (Jeremiah 15:19).

Jeremiah returned to the LORD, finding there the reason to speak the words the LORD wanted him to speak to these people. The prophet responded with recommitment, the second principle. God called Jeremiah to be his spokesperson. Jeremiah expressed his gratitude for his forgiveness by striving to be the best spokesperson possible. Filled with joy over God's mercy, Jeremiah worked to stifle all conceit that he knew more than the LORD did about the direction his life should take. He replaced his thoughts with God's thoughts, with thoughts from God's Word. He honored his Creator as the Potter. He took comfort in being clay in the hands of his loving LORD.

> God's gracious forgiveness in Christ and his promises of eternal life prompt us to recommit ourselves to desire God's leadership in our lives.

Recommitment works the same for us. God's gracious forgiveness in Christ and his promises of eternal life prompt us to recommit ourselves to desire God's leadership in our lives. We tell him we want to remain committed to honoring his potter role in our lives. We ask him to empower us to trust him as the ultimate authority in our lives. We recommit ourselves to his promises even when they seem impossible.

We seek to lay hold of Jeremiah's confession: "[Your] compassions never fail. They are new every morning; great is your faithfulness. I say to myself, 'The LORD is my portion; therefore I will wait for him'" (Lamentations 3:22-24).

Response

"I will make you a wall to this people," God promised Jeremiah, "a fortified wall of bronze; they will fight against you but will not overcome you" (Jeremiah 15:20).

God committed himself to turn Jeremiah into the strongest wall known at that time: an impenetrable metal wall forged from copper and tin alloy. But Jeremiah needed to take God's promise to heart and translate it into his life. A bronze wall is of no protection if it is not put into place.

> God's Jesus-won forgiveness calls us to respond in trust, to act.

God's Jesus-won forgiveness calls us to respond in trust, to act on our position as bronze walls. That's the third principle. We are asked to do what the priests did on the shores of the flooding Jordan River. When the Israelites were about to cross into the Promised Land after 40 years in the wilderness, the LORD instructed the priests to carry the ark of the covenant into the Jordan. Then he commanded, "When you reach the edge of the Jordan's waters, go and stand in the river" (Joshua 3:8).

Walking into a river at flood stage invites drowning. But the priests stepped into the river as God commanded. At that instant, the Jordan stopped flowing. They—and God's people—crossed the river on dry ground (see Joshua chapter 3).

God also calls us to respond to his grace by stepping into the floodwaters. Jesus shouted, "It is finished," from the cross. That shout assures us that he will work miracles to honor his promises. God's commitment to us calls on us to overrule our thoughts about how we have a better way, a safer way, a less demanding way to direct our lives. He calls us to live as the piece of pottery he—in his love for us—has shaped us to be. He invites us to put our faith in him—our recommitment to his promises—into actions. Thinking of his promises. Sharing his promises. Living in confidence because of those promises.

Wait quietly for the salvation of the LORD

Jeremiah does no little complaining in the book of Lamentations. Yet among the laments are clear words of repentance, recommitment, and response. He provides us with a confession we can use whenever our thinking strays from our Creator's thinking. Here are words to help us regain our balance when bellyaching has left us on the shore rather than strolling across the Jordan's dry riverbed.

> I say to myself, "The LORD is my portion; therefore I will wait for him." The LORD is good to those whose hope is in him, to the one who seeks him; it is good to wait quietly for the salvation of the LORD.
>
> It is good for a man to bear the yoke while he is young. Let him sit alone in silence, for the LORD has laid it on him. Let him bury his face in the dust—there may yet be hope. Let him offer his cheek to one who would strike him, and let him be filled with disgrace.
>
> For no one is cast off by the Lord forever. Though he brings grief, he will show compassion, so great is his unfailing love. For he does not willingly bring affliction or grief to anyone. (Lamentations 3:24-33)

"The LORD is my portion." The Hebrew word translated as "portion" described the land allotted to God's people when they conquered Canaan under Joshua. It named the spoils of war that the Israelites captured from the Canaanites. It also identified the part of the sacrifices that God allowed the priests to keep for themselves.

We are patient while the LORD reveals his plans for our lives because he is our portion. He has allotted to us a certain parcel of life on this planet. He has shared with us the spoils of his Son's Easter triumph. He has given us the full benefit of Jesus' Good Friday sacrifice.

> We are patient while the LORD reveals his plans for our lives.

For those reasons, we joyfully wait for him to help us because we know how good he is. We wait quietly because he has saved us from the consequences of our sins. We find strength to go on, even when the burdens of life are heavy, because "no one is cast off by the Lord forever." He will show us compassion. We will enjoy his unfailing love. And we will find comfort in knowing that our troubles never come from a divine heart that enjoys seeing us suffer.

Take a moment now to pledge that you will trust your Father rather than yourself. And if your resolve fails? Then like Jeremiah, begin again with repentance, recommitment, and response.

Prayer

Gracious Father, I shudder to think of the blessings I have missed because I trusted my judgment about the best way to direct my life rather than your judgment. Cancer was never a part of my life plan, but you chose to include it. For the faithless complaining I have done, please forgive me.

Fill me with the joy of your salvation so that I recommit myself to following your direction for my life. Then inspire me to say with Jeremiah, "The LORD is my portion; therefore I will wait for him." Based on the guarantees certified in Jesus, bring me to respond to your promises with obedience and trust. Amen.

Chapter 6
DO I TALK MORE THAN I LISTEN?

In the late 1970s, comedian Gilda Radner developed the character Emily Litella for *Saturday Night Live* (SNL). Dowdy in dress, outspoken in style, and impaired in hearing, Emily Litella was portrayed as a guest commentator on SNL's Weekend Update.

Ms. Litella inveighed against outrageous social evils. Or at least what her poor hearing led her to believe were social evils. "What is all this fuss I hear about the Supreme Court decision on a 'deaf' penalty?" she screeched. "It's terrible! Deaf people have enough problems as it is!"

Her outrage would flare as she vilified the proponents of the nonexistent injustice she championed. When she would pause to catch her breath, the news anchor would jump into the conversation. "That's death penalty, Ms. Litella, not deaf . . . death." Her error exposed, Ms. Litella would say, "Oh, that's very different . . ." Then with a bemused smile, she would say, "Never mind."

Emily Litella is an example of what happens when we express our opinions without understanding the situation. How often we react to what God is doing without understanding his plan and forgetting the dominant attitude of love for us.

"Never mind" moments

Jeremiah has his moments. He complained about injustice even though God had spoken to him over the decades of his ministry. In chapter after chapter of Jeremiah's book, God had explained that he would destroy Jerusalem and why. Yet in the smoldering, bloodstained ruins of the city, Jeremiah mounted a soapbox. There he derided God for unfairly punishing Jerusalem.

Look, LORD, and consider: Whom have you ever treated like this? Should women eat their offspring, the children they have cared for? Should priest and prophet be killed in the sanctuary of the Lord?

Young and old lie together in the dust of the streets; my young men and young women have fallen by the sword. You have slain them in the day of your anger; you have slaughtered them without pity. As you summon to a feast day, so you summoned against me terrors on every side. In the day of the LORD's anger no one escaped or survived; those I cared for and reared my enemy has destroyed. (Lamentations 2:20-22)

How could Jeremiah write that? How could he challenge God for the judgment the LORD himself foretold? Did he forget God's promises? Wasn't God's judgment just? Did Jeremiah want to excuse the people and ask God to withhold his judgment?

> [Jeremiah] shifted dramatically from complaining to a confident trust in the LORD's great love.

The complaint is all Jeremiah wrote. But he soon shifted dramatically from complaining to a confident trust in the LORD's great love. The next chapter records one of those "never mind" moments. Jeremiah wrote, "Yet this I call to mind and therefore I have hope: Because of the LORD's great love we are not consumed, for his compassions never fail" (Lamentations 3:21,22). Never mind about my complaint. I trust the LORD.

Jeremiah chapter 20 gives us another example of the prophet's complaint mixed with confidence in the LORD. He complains, "You deceived me, LORD, and I was deceived; . . . I am ridiculed all day long; everyone mocks me" (Jeremiah 20:7). But he also confesses, "The LORD is with me like a mighty warrior" (Jeremiah 20:11).

Then Jeremiah tells us to sing, "Sing to the LORD! Give praise to the LORD! He rescues the life of the needy from the hands of the wicked" (Jeremiah 20:13). He's not done yet with complaining. Listen to the next verse: "Cursed be the day I was born! May the day my mother bore me not be blessed!" (Jeremiah 20:14). He continues that complaint until the end of the chapter, concluding, "Why did I ever come out of the womb to see trouble and sorrow and to end my days in shame?" (Jeremiah 20:18).

As Jeremiah shifted between complaint and faith, the LORD often encouraged him with great promises. One of them comes shortly after these verses. God speaks a promise of the coming Savior: "The days are coming, . . . when I will raise up for David a righteous Branch, a King who will reign wisely and do what is just and right in the land. In his days Judah will be saved and Israel will live in safety. This is the name by which he will be called: The LORD Our Righteous Savior" (Jeremiah 23:5,6).

> As Jeremiah shifted between complaint and faith, the LORD often encouraged him with great promises.

God is so patient. Confronted with the destruction, death, and pain of the devastation of Jerusalem and Judah, Jeremiah is human. He saw it all first in God's threats and then later in reality as he saw the smoke and the heaps of rubble. It troubled him enough to complain and challenge God's choices. Then he had a "never mind" moment when he spoke in faith and remembered God's persistent and everlasting love for all humanity.

Did you catch it? A blessing endures even when we complain to God about his plans for our lives. The blessing? All the promises he has made. They are all wrapped up in the righteous Branch of David—Jesus. They are real and permanent. As we look at our own situation, we, like Jeremiah, flip-flop from complaint to trust. Complaining should pave the road to a forehead slap and the exclamation "What am I doing? How am I in a position to instruct my Father about what is best for me? Think about his promises. I need to stop talking and start listening."

Feedback loops

We who battle cancer can concentrate so much on trying to help God understand our predicament—as though he needs our help—that we fail to understand what he is telling us. When that happens, we create a feedback loop that intensifies our grumbling the more we complain.

That happened to Emily Litella. And to Jeremiah. We become victims of that feedback loop phenomenon whenever we are more interested in hearing ourselves complain than we are in listening to our God speak.

You've heard that loud, screeching noise that happens when feedback overtakes a sound system. Feedback loops occur when a microphone picks up an amplified sound from the speakers. That amplified sound feeds back into the audio system where it is reamplified. Then the microphone picks up the even louder sound. It is sent into the sound system and back out of the speakers where it once again enters the microphone. It all happens so quickly. The cycle continues until all the audio system can produce is ear-shattering shrieks.

When we are content to complain without paying attention to God's voice, those complaints create feedback. They amplify in volume until there is only overpowering noise. In the end, all we hear are our complaints. They are no longer rational. They are no longer connected to faith. They are screeches that drown out God's voice of grace and reason.

A breast cancer survivor described how that feedback loop worked in her life.

I do remember getting blue. I gave up my job last summer. It was just a no brainer. I would have been an HR nightmare. I didn't feel any question about my decision to do that, but I still felt a stupid guilt.

I compared myself with others with cancer. This person is getting up every morning and dragging herself to work despite all she had to do. And I'm not doing that.

I think I did quite a bit of that. Even with all the gratitude for my blessings, I felt guilt for not handling my cancer better. And I felt guilt because I didn't feel as strong as other women with cancer.

The citizens of Jeremiah's Jerusalem got caught in a feedback loop. They chose to complain about God's apparent unfairness rather than to listen to his instruction. The LORD warned of the calamitous consequences, "I am bringing disaster on this people, the fruit of their schemes, because they have not listened to my words and have rejected my law" (Jeremiah 6:19, see also Jeremiah 6:17; 7:13,26; 11:10; 25:4,7). Unfortunately, the squeals of that feedback loop overpowered God's message.

The fix for feedback loops

But there is a solution. It's the same solution that remedies a screaming sound system: Turn off the microphone. Stop feeding complaints into the system. Be quiet. Don't say another word. *Listen.*

The people of Jerusalem struggled with that solution. Even after the Babylonians captured the city and took thousands into exile, God's people complained rather than listened. The city was destroyed a full decade later, but the people were more interested in their own perceptions than in their Father's call to repentance and faith.

How could the people have canceled the feedback screech? By shutting off their complaints. Then they needed to listen to their

God. The LORD said, "They have not listened to my words . . . I sent to them again and again by my servants the prophets. And you exiles have not listened either." Then Jeremiah encouraged, "Hear the word of the LORD, all you exiles whom I have sent away from Jerusalem to Babylon" (Jeremiah 29:19,20).

> "Take a breath and listen to me" is a refrain throughout the Scriptures.

"Take a breath and listen to me" is a refrain throughout the Scriptures. Psalm 46:2 imagines the earth giving way and the mountains falling into the heart of the sea. But the psalmist urges us to heed God's exhortation: "Be still, and know that I am God." The reason? Because he will keep his promises and we will reap the benefit. "I will be exalted among the nations, I will be exalted in the earth," our Father vows (Psalm 46:10). Our response to upheaval is a shout of victory: "The LORD Almighty is with us; the God of Jacob is our fortress" (Psalm 46:11).

Note that it is the LORD who is with us. Because our God of full and free grace has shown that we can trust him—even when we can't understand him—we give up our fretting and are quiet.

Blessed is the one who trusts in the LORD

"I will be exalted," God says (Psalm 46:10). How do we know that in the end—no matter what injustice prompts our complaints, no matter how torturous our cancer—God will be exalted? Because his Word promises that.

He has founded his promises on his Son's death in our place and on the guarantees of Jesus' resurrection. Since Jesus died and rose again, all of God's promises are secured. That's the apostle's point in 2 Corinthians 1:20: "No matter how many promises God has made, they are 'Yes' in Christ."

Isn't that the reason God told Jeremiah, "Cursed is the one who trusts in man, who draws strength from mere flesh and whose heart turns away from the LORD. But blessed is the one who trusts in the LORD, whose confidence is in him. They will be like a tree planted by the water that sends out its roots by the stream" (Jeremiah 17:5,7,8)?

What assurance! Reject depending on your own wisdom. Reject misinformed, Emily-Litella-like complaining. Instead, sink your roots into the Bible's water of life. Drink from the quiet stream of the Spirit's Word. Be invigorated by its promises. Listening to the Scriptures is the cure for incessant complaining.

> He has founded his promises on his Son's death in our place and on the guarantees of Jesus' resurrection.

God's Word always accomplishes our Father's loving desires for us and achieves his eternal purposes (Isaiah 55:11).

In Jude's epistle, the Spirit encourages us to listen rather than complain. Jude's audience faced upheaval in the congregation. It came from "ungodly people" who "secretly slipped in among" the people (Jude 4). But don't let this upset you, Jude says. And don't follow their example. "These people are grumblers and faultfinders; they follow their own evil desires" (Jude 16). Rather, Jude continues, give yourself to growing in your knowledge of the Scriptures. "You, dear friends, by building yourselves up in your most holy faith and praying in the Holy Spirit, keep yourselves in God's love as you wait for the mercy of our Lord Jesus Christ to bring you to eternal life" (Jude 20,21).

We build our trust in God's plans for our lives and assure ourselves of God's love through listening to God speak to us in his Word. Consider Romans 10:17: "Faith comes from hearing the message, and the message is heard through the word about Christ." Consider Jesus' words in Luke 11:28: "Blessed rather are those who hear the word of God and obey it." Consider Psalm 119:105: "Your word is a lamp for my feet, a light on my path."

We shut down the feedback loop that our complaining generates when we pull the plug on our complaints. In the silence that results, we give our attention to our Father's tender truths.

Dwelling in God's Word

We have many ways to explore God's Word. First to mind are the opportunities our church offers for worship and Bible study. Our own personal Bible reading comes a close second. Devotion times with our families and small group Bible studies with friends are also important.

But paying attention to our Father is not just taking his words into our minds through our eyes or ears. It's meditating on them, singing them, praying them back to him. It's taking them into our hearts and assimilating them into our lives. It's becoming a tree that "sends out its roots by the stream," a tree that never ceases to yield fruit (Jeremiah 17:8).

Patience

When we drink fully of the Scriptures, two blessings replace our complaints.

We learn how to wait for God to act. We learn patience, the first blessing. We learn how to trust God to act in grace, just as he promised he would. The LORD called Jeremiah to such a trust. "I am the LORD," he reminded his prophet. "I am the LORD, who exercises kindness, justice and righteousness on earth, for in these I delight" (Jeremiah 9:24). No matter how Jeremiah misinterpreted the events happening around him, the LORD would remain kind, just, and righteous. God intended that Jeremiah's continuing contact with the Word would drum that refrain into the prophet's head and heart.

Some songs stick in our heads, playing and replaying in an unending loop. Usually, these earworms annoy. But as we struggle with cancer's assaults, we need the earworm of God's gospel playing in our hearts. We need the continuing reminder that regardless of the cacophony crashing in our ears, everything is under our wise Father's control. We need to hear the symphony of Jesus' life, death, resurrection, and ascension. This music assures us that our God is faithful and good. We need ceaseless reminders that these events are facts of history. Facts cannot be changed; their impact cannot be undone. Therefore, God's commitment to us is changeless.

To transform our complaints into praise doesn't come with occasional sips from the Bible's life-giving stream. It requires bathing in the Scriptures. Luxuriating in them. Hour after hour. Until we come out wrinkled, transformed by their soothing touch.

During Wisconsin's long, cold January nights, we upper Midwesterners would never think of snuggling into bed with a 1-square-foot blanket as our bedcover. We want a substantial, king-sized, down-filled comforter. Even better, we want a comforter with an electric heater. We want a blanket large enough to cover our toes and tuck tightly under our chins.

Listening to God's Word requires the same head-to-toe wrapping. Only then are we protected from life's cold chill. Only then are we adequately warmed by God's grace. A raggedy scrap of muslin won't suffice.

John encouraged us to snuggle into that grace when he wrote, "See what great love the Father has lavished on us, that we should be called children of God!" (1 John 3:1). *See* might also be translated as "experience, perceive, or discern." Wrap yourself completely in the Father's love; experience it fully.

Jeremiah was able to see the great love God had lavished on him. Yes, the events of Jesus' ministry lay six centuries in the future. That did not matter. God had promised this adoption belonged to Jeremiah. The coming Messiah would sign the adoption papers. That grace positioned Jeremiah to quietly await the LORD's deliverance.

Remember the LORD's promise of "a righteous Branch" (Jeremiah 23:5). We are on the other side of the Messiah's coming. "The LORD Our Righteous Savior" appeared on our planet two thousand years ago (Jeremiah 23:6). The grace we see lived out in Jesus is the Gibraltar Rock upon which each promise of God rests. "Because of his great love for us, God, who is rich in mercy, made us alive with Christ even when we were dead in transgressions" (Ephesians 2:4,5). Since he's done that, his commitment to us in every other area of life is guaranteed. We are empowered to face cancer or any trial with patience.

Direction for life

That brings us to the second blessing. Because Jesus guarantees God will keep his promises, we not only find patience in God's Word but we also find direction for dealing with life's upheavals.

Through Jeremiah, the LORD told his people, "Let not the wise boast of their wisdom or the strong boast of their strength or the rich boast of their riches, but let the one who boasts boast about this: that they have the understanding to know me, that I am the LORD, who exercises kindness, justice and righteousness on earth, for in these I delight" (Jeremiah 9:23,24).

> We complain when we know better than God.

We complain when we boast in our own wisdom, strength, or wealth. We complain when we know better than God. We complain when we have a superior plan.

Our complaining ceases when God's grace gives us something more solid to boast about: the knowledge of his will for us. Only in God's Word do we find "the understanding to know . . . the LORD." Only in God's Word can we discover that "the LORD . . . exercises kindness, justice and righteousness on earth" (Jeremiah 9:24).

Proverbs 2:6,9-11 says, "The LORD gives wisdom; from his mouth come knowledge and understanding. Then you will understand what is right and just and fair—every good path. For wisdom will enter your heart, and knowledge will be pleasant to your soul. Discretion will protect you, and understanding will guard you."

Swaddled in the Scriptures, we find direction for our lives. "He guides me along the right paths for his name's sake," David says of the LORD and his Word. "Even though I walk through the darkest valley, I will fear no evil, for you are with me; your rod and your staff, they comfort me" (Psalm 23:3,4).

Finding a way through life has enough challenges without cancer's roadblocks. I am three years past the chemotherapy that battled the cancer cells that remained in the area of my prostate. Every PSA test since then has demonstrated that I am cancer free. But every six months, before I have another test, fears that the cancer may have returned haunt me.

Uncertainty is part of being a cancer survivor. It's part of the thick of the battle. The worries are never pushed away for long. "Is the cancer completely gone? Will it return? Among the various options, what is the most effective treatment? Should I stop receiving treatment? How will my family deal with my disease?"

In the face of those questions, God speaks to us in his Word to calm our fears and overcome our worries. He reminds us that he is "the LORD, who exercises kindness, justice and righteousness on earth, for in these [he delights]" (Jeremiah 9:24). He assures us that his Son Jesus is the "King who will reign wisely and do what is just and right in the land. . . . The LORD Our Righteous Savior" (Jeremiah 23:5,6). He confirms that he will guide us through the darkest of valleys and provide us with such secure delight that we can feast in the face of fear.

The LORD guided Jeremiah through his tumultuous ministry. He promised his prophet, "I will make you a wall to this people, a fortified wall of bronze; they will fight against you but will not overcome you, for I am with you to rescue and save you" (Jeremiah 15:20). God kept that promise even when Jeremiah was imprisoned, beaten, falsely accused, plotted against, and ridiculed.

Listen to Jeremiah again as he flip-flops but has that "never mind" moment. I think you can identify with him and his words in your struggle with cancer: "I have been deprived of peace; I have forgotten what prosperity is. So I say, 'My splendor is gone and all that I had hoped from the LORD.' I remember my affliction and my wandering, the bitterness and the gall. I well remember them, and my soul is downcast within me" (Lamentations 3:17-20). Been there!

But don't stay there. Jeremiah goes on, "Yet this I call to mind and therefore I have hope: Because of the LORD's great love we are not consumed, for his compassions never fail. They are new every morning; great is your faithfulness. I say to myself, 'The LORD is my potion; therefore I will wait for him'" (Lamentations 3:21-24). Been there too!

The Scriptures proclaim that those promises belong to every believer. They belong to us. "Do not fear, for I am with you," God tells us. "Do not be dismayed, for I am your God. I will strengthen you and help you; I will uphold you with my righteous right hand" (Isaiah 41:10). We trust his guidance: "The LORD is my rock, my fortress and my deliverer; my God is my rock, in whom I take refuge, my shield and the horn of my salvation, my stronghold" (Psalm 18:2).

That prompts us to pray, "Since you are my rock and my fortress, for the sake of your name lead and guide me" (Psalm 31:3). LORD, you have promised, "I know the plans I have for you, . . . plans to prosper you and not to harm you, plans to give you hope and a future" (Jeremiah 29:11). Those plans are far better than anything I can imagine. Change my heart so I am willing to follow wherever you lead. Keep me humble before you, awed by your love and wisdom.

God's love notes

Abraham Lincoln said, "Better to remain silent and be thought a fool than to speak out and remove all doubt."

In any social situation, talking more than we listen is a recipe for embarrassment or worse. That recipe produces a more unsavory dish when we talk to God more than we listen to him.

Doctors diagnosed my father's pancreatic cancer a week before Thanksgiving in 1997. They predicted he would live for 6 to 12 months. The news devastated me. Outside of some hearing loss, my 75-year-old father enjoyed good health. My assumption that he would gracefully live into his 80s, or perhaps 90s, shattered. On some level God was to blame.

But my "never mind" moment came eventually. I required several months to appreciate the bouquet of blessings that came to me through Dad's death in March 1998. I came to realize my grief made me more empathetic toward the grieving people to whom I ministered. Dad provided me with an amazing lesson in how Christians face death. Those months gave me a special opportunity (one I had not taken full advantage of) to tell my father what he meant to me and how much I loved him. Most important, I learned more fully to trust my Father in heaven with the lives of my loved ones—and my own life.

> But complaining is always a means to an end for us Christians. It's a signal that we need to be quiet and listen to our Father speak to us.

The Scriptures do not fault us for expressing our exasperation to God. Quite the opposite—they encourage it. But complaining is always a means to an end for us Christians. It's a signal that we need to be quiet and listen to our Father speak to us.

The LORD has a book filled with his love notes to you. Open it up. Hear what he has to say to you. Let it shape your thoughts, fill your heart, and transform your life.

You'll be much happier listening to him talk with you than you will be grousing to him. Especially when that conversation ends with Emily Littela's "Never mind."

Prayer

Father, when I complain, I talk more than I listen. Unfortunately, the more I talk without listening to you, the more confused I become. Since nothing in all creation "will be able to separate us from the love of God that is in Christ Jesus our Lord" (Romans 8:39), lead me to listen rather than complain.

This is hard for me to say, but thank you. Thank you because you are using this disease to encourage me to immerse myself in your Word. Thank you because cancer invites me to hear your gospel's comfort with new ears. Thank you. Amen.

Chapter 7
MY SOURCE OF STRENGTH

My youngest grandkids and I share a jar-opening ritual.

Each round begins when my wife asks me, "Honey, would you open this jar of jelly?" Of course, the game also works with jars of mustard, olives, salsa, sauerkraut—anything sealed in a jar.

I hand the jar to one of the grandkids. "Would you open this jar for Nana?" I ask.

They hold the jar as tightly as their preschool fingers allow. Their fingertips whiten. Their faces redden. Their lips, pursed in determination, fade from burnished ruby to bleary rose.

After wrestling the cover without success, they hand the jar back to me. Defeat droops their shoulders. They concede, "I can't do it, Papa." Sometimes the game takes an unwanted turn at this point. A three-year-old's frustration at an impossible task results in tears.

"That must be a tough one," I say. "What if we try this together?"

Little hands once again grasp the jar. Papa-hands envelope them. "Are you ready?" I ask. "One. Two. Three. Twist." With a slight pop, the seal breaks and the lid comes free.

I'm always pleased with the delight that beams across their face.

"Great job!" I cheer. "You really are strong."

I have it handled

The Almighty does something similar—but more profound—in our lives when he allows obstacles to block our paths. He presents us with a problem that is impossible for us to solve. Like my grandkids, we go to our heavenly Father asking for help. Often he challenges us to grapple with our predicament. He wants us to be strengthened or to learn from our struggle. Then he congratulates us on the triumph he worked: "Well done, good and faithful servant!" (Matthew 25:23). But our success would have never happened without his power.

Having cancer is similar to holding an immense jar of jelly in our too-tiny hands. We struggle with it. Sometimes it's just to get through the day or the pain. Sometimes it's fighting for strength to overcome the weariness. The challenges are many, but we realize they require more strength than we possess.

This chapter deals with negotiating the intersection of trusting God's power to overcome what is beyond us and understanding that God chooses to involve us in conquering those challenges.

Open the jelly jar

We complain because the Himalayas in our lives seem beyond our ability to scale. Usually that happens because we are looking to our own resources rather than God's. The Almighty pointed out to Jeremiah that he had fallen into that trap.

From the beginning, Jeremiah realized that the task God gave him was beyond his abilities. Yet the LORD promised, "I am with you and will rescue you" (Jeremiah 1:19). The LORD had not twisted the lid quickly enough to suit Jeremiah. Throughout the land, evil seethed like the mudpots in Yellowstone National Park. But nothing the prophet did lowered the temperature of that bubbling evil.

The LORD explained to Jeremiah and Jerusalem why the Babylonian disaster would happen: "From the time I brought your ancestors up from Egypt until today, I warned them again and again, saying, 'Obey me.' But they did not listen or pay attention; instead, they followed the stubbornness of their evil hearts. So I brought on them all the curses of the covenant I had commanded them to follow but that they did not keep" (Jeremiah 11:7,8). Destruction was at the door. The door could not be barred.

A dozen verses later, God's vow to penalize his people led him to command Jeremiah, "Do not pray for this people or offer any plea or petition for them, because I will not listen when they call to me in the time of their distress" (Jeremiah 11:14).

A struggle with frustration

But God's failure to bring that justice on Jerusalem frustrated the prophet. He had preached about it. He had predicted it. But God's punishment hadn't happened. In chapter 12, Jeremiah complains.

> You are always righteous, LORD, when I bring a case before you. Yet I would speak with you about your justice: Why does the way of the wicked prosper? Why do all the faithless live at ease?

> You have planted them, and they have taken root; they grow and bear fruit. You are always on their lips but far from their hearts.

> Yet you know me, LORD; you see me and test my thoughts about you.

> Drag them off like sheep to be butchered! Set them apart for the day of slaughter! How long will the land lie parched and the grass in every field be withered? Because those who live in it are wicked, the animals and birds have perished. Moreover, the people are saying, "He will not see what happens to us." (Jeremiah 12:1-4)

We have noted the prophet's tussle between complaint and trust. He began by acknowledging, "You are always righteous, LORD, when I bring a case before you." But his trust immediately vanishes. He reverts to haranguing God for not doing the right thing soon enough: "Why does the way of the wicked prosper? Why do all the faithless live at ease? You know me, LORD; you see me and test my thoughts about you" (Jeremiah 12:1,3). That is, I've been faithful to you. I deserve better treatment than this.

> We have noted the prophet's tussle between complaint and trust.

Has cancer made you familiar with this struggle? Have you demanded that God act immediately to heal you? Like Jeremiah, have you felt that God has defaulted in paying his debt to you or even answering your prayers?

In Jeremiah's mind, he had been a strong force for God in Israel. He had worked hard. He had even put his life on the line. He had fulfilled his end of the bargain. God had reneged on his obligation. God had failed to act as the prophet anticipated.

Jeremiah viewed himself as the faithful employee who was not paid. The prophet demanded his boss' justice: "Drag them off like sheep to be butchered! Set them apart for the day of slaughter!" (Jeremiah 12:3).

The source of power

I never play the jelly jar game with my grandkids to discourage them. On rare occasions, however, the game veers in that direction. When the jar doesn't open, their frustrations may flare. They tried with all their might to twist off the lid, but it wasn't enough. At those times, the experience reduces them to a sobbing heap in the middle of the kitchen floor.

I wonder how close cancer has brought you to that kitchen floor. The enormity of dealing with cancer usually brings tears along with fears. The realization that the jar won't open no matter how hard we try seems unfair.

Jeremiah's firmly sealed jar frustrated him. He should have been frustrated. He was looking in the wrong place for the power to twist open the seal and succeed. Justice would not depend on Jeremiah's effort or worthiness.

The LORD asks, "If you have raced with men on foot and they have worn you out, how can you compete with horses? If you stumble in safe country, how will you manage in the thickets by the Jordan?" (Jeremiah 12:5).

Let me tell you about the amount of strength you bring to this situation, God says. You think you are strong, Jeremiah? You haven't experienced anything to test your strength. The coming events will be much worse. These days are like a footrace; the hardship to come will be like racing against horses. These days are like a walk in the country; the trials to come will be like trail blazing through the tangled jungles along the Jordan River. My son, if you haven't learned it yet, you need to learn it now. To open this jar requires more strength than you can find in yourself.

I will fix this, God tells his spokesperson. That day is coming. I promised it; it will happen. "I will forsake my house, abandon my inheritance; I will give the one I love into the hands of her enemies. They will bear the shame of their harvest because of the LORD's fierce anger" (Jeremiah 12:7,13). But the LORD would not stop there. In all these threats of punishment, don't miss the promise of God's grace for the Israelites and their neighbors. The LORD assures that when his justice has run its course, he will show undeserved love to his people and their enemies: "After I uproot them, I will again have compassion" (Jeremiah 12:15).

I will bring justice, the LORD insists. I have the power and the will. Your role in my plan is to be faithful to my instruction. The outcome is not in your hands. It can't be. It's beyond your pay grade. So, my dear son, give up your frustration. I have this handled. I will keep my promises. I will bring justice. I will open the jar. I will demonstrate my mercy. All in the way I determine. All at the time I determine.

"Be still before the LORD and wait patiently for him," King David wrote four hundred years before Jeremiah. "Do not fret when people succeed in their ways, when they carry out their wicked schemes" (Psalm 37:7). The reason for such patient waiting for God to act on his promises? "The salvation of the righteous comes from the LORD; he is their stronghold in time of trouble. The LORD helps them and delivers them; he delivers them from the wicked and saves them, because they take refuge in him" (Psalm 37:39,40).

> Cancer seems unjust. Especially for people who are living in a committed relationship with Jesus.

Cancer seems unjust. Especially for people who are living in a committed relationship with Jesus. We are like Jeremiah. That sense of injustice heightens when God apparently reneges on his commitment to heal us.

"Wait patiently," David advises. God remains your stronghold. He will help and deliver you. Among all the Old Testament heroes of faith, David stands out as one who had a lifetime of experience with enemies. He also discovered that "the salvation of the righteous comes from the LORD." No matter how disappointed you are with God, David advises, "Take refuge in him."

This is how God answers another objection. We say to God, "Why did you allow this to happen, Father? Why did you hand me a sealed jelly jar that I can't open? I can't make sense of what you are doing."

Why does God allow us to struggle?

At the heart of this complaint is our assumption that God's infinite wisdom will always make sense to our finite intellect. How illogical that assumption! Because of "the depth of the riches of the wisdom and knowledge of God," his judgments are unsearchable "and his paths beyond tracing out!" No human being is able to know "the mind of the Lord" or be his counselor (Romans 11:33,34).

Yet we often think that God would do well to take our advice.

And when we assume that, our frustration with God rises because he always has other ideas. In frustration, we may want to push his jelly jar away or break it on the floor. Then we miss out on the good things our wise God intended to accomplish. Consider what the people Jeremiah preached to would have missed if he had refused to "wait patiently" and "take refuge" in the LORD (Psalm 37:7,40). Consider what we would have missed if we had no record of Jeremiah's struggles and successes.

Now consider your cancer. The reasons God allows it probably do not seem reasonable. But we don't have to understand why God allows trouble in our lives. What we need to understand is that the almighty LORD is eternally committed to love and care for us. Jesus shows that "the salvation of the righteous comes from the LORD; he is their stronghold in time of trouble" (Psalm 37:39).

> What we need to understand is that the almighty LORD is eternally committed to love and care for us.

That truth allows us to confess with Jeremiah, "Great and mighty God, whose name is the LORD Almighty, great are your purposes and mighty are your deeds" (Jeremiah 32:18,19). In our struggles, we have no idea what God is working to accomplish, but we know he is the LORD Almighty and find comfort there.

So put your hands back on the jar lid. Feel your Father's mighty hands around yours. Give that jar another twist.

Celebrate helplessness

Twist the lid. Those are easy words to put on a page. They are hard to put into our lives.

Cancer makes us feel helpless. One response is anger with God. A better response is celebrating our helplessness.

As counterintuitive as that seems, helplessness is worth celebrating. It's a treasure because it forces us to look away from our resources to our Father's.

A friend of mine was one of the most health-conscious people I've ever known. He ate all the right foods. He exercised regularly. He schooled himself about healthy living. But none of that was a match for cancer. The disease quickly robbed him of his strength and left him helpless.

In one of our last devotions before he died, we considered Psalm 121:1,2. A helpless psalmist writes, "I lift up my eyes to the mountains—where does my help come from?" Then he answers his own question, "My help comes from the LORD, the Maker of heaven and earth."

The source of our help is the God whose name is the LORD (Yahweh). His name testifies that he is the God of limitless love for sin-corrupted humans. He is the God who would sacrifice himself to provide us with forgiveness. Not only does he love us beyond any measure we can imagine, but he also has the power to help us.

For proof of God's power, look to creation, the psalmist says. The LORD is the one who called the vast, complex universe into existence in six 24-hour days. That omnipotent being is the one who helps us. Psalm 121:2 says, "[Our] help comes from the LORD, the Maker of heaven and earth."

God has given us a limitless treasure in his commitment to use his power and love for our benefit. I love my children and grandchildren. I would willingly die for them, but I don't have the money, position, or influence to provide them with everything they need. I love them, but I don't have the power to exercise that love as I would like. That makes me remarkably different from our Father in heaven. He is never bound by any limits—not to his power or love.

"I will forsake my house, abandon my inheritance; I will give the one I love into the hands of her enemies," the LORD said of his people (Jeremiah 12:7). "After I uproot them, I will again have compassion" (Jeremiah 12:15). God assured Jeremiah that he had the power and love to do what he promised. God told his spokesperson, "Dry your tears. Pick yourself up from the kitchen floor. Put your hands back on the jar. Let's do this together."

The jelly jar lesson that God gave Jeremiah transformed his complaining spokesperson. In the midst of Jeremiah's lament over his demolished city, the prophet acknowledged,

> I called on your name, LORD, from the depths of the pit. You heard my plea: "Do not close your ears to my cry for relief." You came near when I called you, and you said, "Do not fear." You, Lord, took up my case; you redeemed my life. (Lamentations 3:55-58)

Jeremiah got it. He learned to trust God's strength rather than his own.

Work with me

That is a lesson for us as well. But there's more to it. It also includes working with God to accomplish what he wants to accomplish through us. Even though our Father has every situation handled, he invites us to work with him. He places his hands over ours to open the jelly jar. We can't do it, but as we struggle, our hands become stronger.

In this chapter, we are dealing with the intersection between trusting the LORD to use his power to rescue us and understanding that he involves us in conquering those challenges. Let's consider how God might intend to strengthen you in your battle with cancer.

We are saved by grace, which Paul emphasized in the first two chapters of Ephesians: "In [Jesus] we have redemption through his blood, the forgiveness of sins, in accordance with the riches of God's grace that he lavished on us" (Ephesians 1:7,8). "Because of his great love for us, God, who is rich in mercy, made us alive with Christ even when we were dead in transgressions—it is by grace you have been saved" (Ephesians 2:4,5).

The apostle goes on to explain that grace has even better news for us. "We are God's handiwork," he adds, "created in Christ Jesus to do good works, which God prepared in advance for us to do" (Ephesians 2:10).

As our almighty Father works to bring every blessing into our lives, we respond with patience. And we are his handiwork, the product of his workmanship, beings he has created. He has placed us into his world for a unique purpose. He has designed us to achieve specific goals for him and his kingdom. He "created in Christ Jesus to do good works, which [he] prepared in advance for us to do."

Partner with God

Let's review. The LORD taught Jeremiah that the power to fulfill his promises rested in his almighty hands. But that did not mean God relegated Jeremiah to be a spectator of his power. The prophet belonged on the field. He had an active role to play.

> In our clash with cancer, God is working with us to provide the blessings he intends for us to enjoy. His challenges drive us to find our strength and comfort in the LORD.

In our clash with cancer, God is working with us to provide the blessings he intends for us to enjoy. His challenges drive us to find our strength and comfort in the LORD. These blessings would not have happened without those challenges. He empowers us to deal with the threats of our cancer, the challenges of our disease, and the turbulence of our treatment.

But God has more for us to do. His power does more than release us from complaining about our disease. It frees us to explore the "good works [he] prepared in advance for us to do" now (Ephesians 2:10). As we struggled, our hands have grown stronger. We have become confident enough to share what we have learned and the strength we have gained.

The LORD kept using Jeremiah to speak to Israel for him. Whether God sent the prophet to the potter's shop (Jeremiah chapter 18), to the real estate agent to buy land (Jeremiah chapter 32), or to an empty water cistern (Jeremiah chapter 38), Jeremiah had a role to fulfill: speak the LORD's threats and gracious promises.

You also have a role to fulfill. Your place is not in the upper deck of the stadium. You are on the starting team. You have plays to run when you visit your doctor, go to work, or spend time with other believers.

We confess God's goodness

Jeremiah used 52 chapters to tell his story of God's promise-keeping. It's a testimony to the LORD's faithfulness in the face of his people's rejection and complaint. We too can use our situation to tell others about God's faithfulness. Like Jeremiah, we can tell about our missteps and God's patient redirection. The Spirit positions us to tell others about how he has soothed our fears and fortified our faith.

When my father was terminally ill, he frequently told others about God's grace. Within a week of his diagnosis and before his condition was public, I drove him to a hardware store. Two of his friends met us in the checkout line.

"Ed, how are you doing?" they asked.

"I have terminal cancer," he said. His friends were stunned into silence. "It's fine," he continued. "I am a Christian. I'm going to heaven."

Four years after my prostatectomy, I received 38 radiation treatments because the cancer returned. For two months, Mondays through Fridays, I sat in a waiting room for my turn to receive treatment. Usually, I would wait with the same people.

"Jim," I told myself, "if you didn't have cancer, you would never have met these folks. God has put you here for a reason. Look for opportunities to talk about God's grace."

Conversations in the waiting room easily moved from "How are you today?" to "Does having cancer make you afraid?" to "May I share with you what keeps me hopeful?" No one refused my witness. Some asked for prayer. I even had a conversation with a devout Muslim man about how Jesus assured me of the Almighty's love.

How is God using your battle with cancer to partner with him?

We repent and start again

We've already discussed the importance of repentance in chapter 5 of this book. We mention it again because learning to trust the LORD's strength rather than our own strength is not a "once mastered, always remembered" lesson.

Jeremiah is an example. He repeatedly lost focus on God's grace. He derided and defied God's plan. Yet in time, he also recognized his errors and confessed them. Then his Father assured him that his love had not eroded.

When God convicts us of our lack of faith, we too have the opportunity to repent. Then empowered by the grace that forgives our sin, we recommit ourselves to live in the joy of our forgiveness. That joy shows itself as we work with our Father on his plans.

Jelly jars

I needed a photo to illustrate this jelly jar idea in a sermon. I arranged a photo shoot with my three-year-old grandson. "Everett, all you have to do is try to twist the lid off," I explained. "You don't have to open the jar. Just try."

With all the might his three-year-old muscles could muster, Everett twisted on the top of the jar.

"Papa, I can't do it," he complained.

"Everett," I assured him, "I didn't ask you to twist off the cover. I only asked you to try to twist the cover off."

God doesn't expect us to do what is beyond our ability. We dare not expect that of ourselves. Our role is to believe him when he tells us, "I have it handled." Our role is to respond when he says, "Work with me. Share how my grace and power have helped you."

Prayer

Father, my cancer has handed me a jelly jar that I cannot open. Teach me to partner with you on opening this jar. Point me to Jesus where I see your limitless power at work. Point me to Jesus where I find the reason to partner with you.

Then as I rejoice in my helplessness, empower me by your grace to await the time you will show how your love and strength have helped me to grow stronger in my faith. Thank you for acting on my prayer for the sake of your Son. Amen.

Chapter 8
MY PRAYER

I rarely feel ready when challenges ambush. But no matter how I feel, God has prepared me.

In June, several years after my first diagnosis, I suddenly developed severe back pain. If I did not sit straight and still, I writhed. If I did not walk stick-tall, my knees buckled. If I did not lie quietly in bed, my spine erupted. I climbed stairs on my hands and knees.

I hobbled into urgent care. My doctor did a thorough exam but was not able to pinpoint a cause. He sent me for X-rays.

When we met 30 minutes later, he said, "Jim, I'd like you to have an MRI. There is a spot on your X-ray that looks suspicious. Now, it's probably nothing. But with your prostate cancer history, we need to learn more."

"Why is that?"

He replied kindly but clearly, "Because prostate cancer can later manifest itself in metastatic spinal disease, cancer in the spine."

"Ah, what? Say that again!" my mind shouted. My face, however, strained to appear unfazed while my mouth said, "I understand. How do I schedule an MRI?" In that moment I realized that either my oncologist did not alert me to the possibility of spinal cancer or I wasn't paying attention when he did. This was new news. I felt bushwhacked.

The MRI happened three weeks later. Then I waited almost a week for the doctor's assessment. Nearly four weeks of wondering what my Father had in mind for me. What a blessing! Let me repeat: What a blessing! On each of those days, God was reminding me that he knew what he was doing in my life. I didn't need to know his plan; all I needed to know was him.

God was preparing me.

> God was reminding me that he knew what he was doing in my life. I didn't need to know his plan; all I needed to know was him.

The result of the MRI? I had arthritis in my spine. I didn't have cancer.

I soon discovered, though, that God had also been preparing me for a second cancer alert.

Four months later, I went for my biannual PSA test to measure the amount of prostate-specific antigens in my body. Because my prostate was removed and the area was later radiated, I should never again have a measurable amount of PSA. If there is a measurable amount of PSA and that amount rises over time, it is a sign that the cancer has returned.

Over six years, a dozen tests indicated that I had less than 0.001 nanograms of PSA per milliliter (ng/mL) of blood. In other words, there were no prostate-specific antigens in my body. My PSA had straight-lined. It seemed dead.

But in November, the PSA test showed that the number had jumped to 0.002 ng/ml.

This number is not a huge increase. It raises only a tinkling of alarm bells. But it does elevate cancer preparedness to the level of watchful waiting: taking no action but staying alert to any additional changes.

"I think this is a lab error," my doctor said. "We could test again in two or three months, but even if the PSA number is at 0.002 or higher, the protocol is that we would still watch and wait."

I sighed when I told her, "Let's wait six months to test again."

Fast-forward to May and the result of my next PSA test. It showed less than 0.001 ng/mL of PSA. No measurable PSA. No cancer.

For more than half a year, the threat of cancer menaced my days. Fortunately, my Father had prepared me for every hour of those days.

- When worry warped my view of life, he encouraged me, "Blessed is the one who trusts in the LORD, whose confidence is in him. They will be like a tree planted by the water that sends out its roots by the stream. It does not fear when heat comes; its leaves are always green. It has no worries in a year of drought and never fails to bear fruit" (Jeremiah 17:7,8).

> When worry warped my view of life, he encouraged me, "Blessed is the one who trusts in the LORD, whose confidence is in him."

- When I complained about the unfairness of my situation, he reminded me that his Son, the LORD our righteous Savior, guarantees that he "will reign wisely and do what is just and right," even though I don't understand his ways (Jeremiah 23:5).
- When I felt deserted and destitute, he whispered, "I have loved you with an everlasting love; I have drawn you with unfailing kindness. I will build you up again" (Jeremiah 31:3,4).

God prepared me for any outcome. He used Jeremiah to mentor me. Jeremiah showed me, even if the cancer had returned, that nothing had changed because the LORD had not changed. Did you catch the irony? God used this book, the book he brought out of me, to drive home to me the same lessons he had taught his prophet.

Of course, he also used my continuing time in his Word, my Christian family, my church, and my believing friends to repeatedly remind me that whether I have cancer or not, my times are in my Savior's hands. My Savior's beautiful, strong, and wise hands. My Savior's hands that bled on the cross for me. My Savior's hands that hold my hands and lead me through life here into life in heaven.

> Every step of the way, my Father continues to prepare me for whatever is next.

Every step of the way, my Father continues to prepare me for whatever is next.

God is also preparing you for whatever is next, including the ambushes. I know that because he has put this book in your hands. Much better, he has put *his* Book in your hands. And he has surrounded you with Christians who remind you of his Word. You are ready to move on, regardless of what the future holds.

"I will make you . . . a fortified wall of bronze," the LORD assured Jeremiah. "I am with you to rescue and save you" (Jeremiah 15:20).

The LORD offers us the same promise. His Son is Immanuel, God with us. His Son is so much "with us" that he became one of us. Immanuel gives us the perfection of his sinless life. As one of us, he shares his Easter victory with us.

My prayer is that through this book, God is preparing you. I pray it has brought you a sharper focus on the promises the LORD has proclaimed to Jeremiah and you. I pray that no matter what awaits in your future and what complaints scream to be heard, like Jeremiah:

- You are driven more deeply into God's Word.
- You find in your Father's love relief from your frustrations and fears.
- You are assured that the LORD walks with you every step of the way—comforting, guiding, and protecting.
- You drown your complaints in the ocean of God's grace.
- You rejoice in your Father's blueprint for your life.

" 'I know the plans I have for you,' declares the LORD, 'plans to prosper you and not to harm you, plans to give you hope and a future' " (Jeremiah 29:11).